The Political

ECPR Press

The ECPR Press is published by the European Consortium for Political Research. It publishes original research from leading political scientists and the best among early career researchers in the discipline. Its scope extends to all fields of political science, international relations and political thought, without restriction in either approach or regional focus. It is also open to interdisciplinary work with a predominant political dimension.

ECPR Press Editors

Editors

Peter Kennealy is Deputy Director of the European University Institute library in Florence, Italy.

Alexandra Segerberg is Associate Professor at the University of Stockholm, Sweden.

Associate Editors

Ian O'Flynn is Senior Lecturer in Political Theory at Newcastle University, UK.

Laura Sudulich is Senior Lecturer in Politics and International Relations at the University of Kent, UK. She is also affiliated to Cevipol (Centre d'Étude de la vie Politique) at the Université libre de Bruxelles.

The Political

Stefano Bartolini

Published by the European Consortium for Political Research, Harbour House, 6–8 Hythe Quay, Colchester, CO2 8JF, United Kingdom

Copyright © 2018 by Stefano Bartolini

All rights reserved. No part of this book may be reproduced in any form or by any electronic or mechanical means, including information storage and retrieval systems, without written permission from the publisher, except by a reviewer who may quote passages in a review.

British Library Cataloguing in Publication Data
A catalogue record for this book is available from the British Library

ISBN: HB 978-1-78660-690-7
ISBN: PB 978-1-78661-309-7

Library of Congress Cataloging-in-Publication Data
Names: Bartolini, Stefano, author.
Title: The political / Stefano Bartolini.
Description: London : ECPR Press, [2018] |
   Includes index.
Identi ers: LCCN 2017052865 (print) | LCCN 2017060084 (ebook) | ISBN
   9781786606914 (electronic) | ISBN 9781786613097 (paperback) | ISBN
9781786606907 (cloth)
Subjects: LCSH: Political science—Philosophy.
Classi ication: LCC JA71 (ebook) | LCC JA71 .B36 2018 (print) | DDC 320.01—dc23
LC record available at https://lccn.loc.gov/2017052865

ecpr.eu/shop

For Niccolò, Emilie, David, Tommaso . . . and Gabriele.

'To be thus is nothing,
But to be safely thus'.

William Shakespeare, *Macbeth*, Act 3, Scene 1

Contents

Preface		ix
Acknowledgements		xv
1	Trajectories of the political	1
2	Nuclear political action	29
3	Conditions for political action: Confinement and monopolisation	61
4	Fields of political action	91
5	What is 'politics'?	117
Afterword		145
Index		147
About the Author		153

Preface

'Politics' is a noun that points to a field or sphere of human activity and interaction. 'Political' is an adjective that usually associates with other names to qualify and specify them. Political behaviour, political institutions, political participation and political groups denote special kinds of behaviour, institutions, participation and groups whose specialty resides in their being 'political'. What does this specification refer to? This is the question that this book aims to answer. I argue that in order to overcome characterisations that focus on mere activities, institutional locations or functions, an inquiry into politics as a field or sphere requires a micro-definition of the distinctive political element in human action. Hence, the emphasis in this book is on 'the political' and on 'political action', leading to an understanding of politics. I believe that this change of perspective is theoretically profitable. It helps to distinguish the changing phenomenology of politics as conventionally understood from its essential and stable core. It may help to more precisely define the knowledge task of the political scientist.

In short, the book is concerned with 'politics' understood as the production and distribution of 'behavioural compliance', as opposed to the view of politics as a distribution of values, an aggregation of preferences or a solution to social dilemmas. Starting from a motivational definition of elementary political action, the endeavour proceeds to a differentiation of compliance instigations in different social fields of interaction, characterised by various levels of confinement of the actors and of monopolisation of command. Eventually, the book concentrates on the single 'meta-good' exclusively and unavoidably reserved for the political: the production of a generalised and stabilised positive attitude towards complying with any possible mechanism of production and distribution of any other good.

The argument unfolds in five chapters. Chapter 1 reviews the development of the terms 'political' and 'politics' in the history of Western thought, in particular in the continual alternation between more vertical and more horizontal conceptions and in the progressive dismembering of them from other spheres of human action such as morality and ethics, religion and society, and law and the state. The chapter also charts the main interpretative conceptions of the political in the twentieth century and concludes by arguing why a continued debate on the subject is necessary and healthy for political science as a discipline.

Chapter 2 introduces my own perspective on the political, centred on an attempt to define the motivation for 'elementary' or 'nuclear' political action as opposed to other elementary actions such as ethical, interest-driven and honour-driven actions. Defining political action as a search for the behavioural compliance of other human beings is rare in the literature, although one can find references to it in the works of some classical scholars. The chapter defends this perspective from the main objections and counterarguments. The most important of these objections is that a 'search for compliance' is too broad a category to specify the distinctive features of the political as it is conventionally understood.

Chapters 3 and 4 face the challenge of differentiating varieties of the search for compliance, nevertheless maintaining that this search always has an inherently political character. In chapter 3, the two main conditions that differentiate the search for compliance in different fields of interaction are identified in the level of 'confinement' of the actors (the extent to which actors involved are bound to interact or are free to leave the interaction) and in the degree of monopolisation of the function of compliance production (the extent to which a field of interaction contains a third actor specialised in the production of compliance). The chapter argues that these two dimensions are fundamental to the differentiation of the search for compliance and are preliminary to any characterisation of different manifestations of the political. A specific combination of the two dimensions – high levels of confinement of actors and monopolisation of command – identifies 'politics' as it is usually and conventionally understood.

Chapter 4 combines the two dimensions of confinement and monopolisation into a fourfold typology of fields of political interaction, each characterised by specific means and forms of compliance production and by the nature of the corresponding final values these forms of compliance can guarantee. The aim of the chapter is to provide a framework that is able to include, and at the same time to significantly differentiate between, the most and the least common forms of the political in the single unifying dimension of the search for and production of behavioural compliance.

In chapter 5, I conclude the argument by moving from political action to politics in general, providing a definition of the latter applicable to the cases which it most commonly refers to, which in my framework include what are defined as the 'authority' and 'governmental' fields of political interaction. Here, my reference points are those conceptions of politics that focus on the aggregation of preferences, on the authoritative allocation of values and on the solution of social dilemmas. Against these visions, I claim that in its most structured forms politics is best characterised by its capacity to produce a single 'political good' in the form of a generalised (for the entire membership group) and stabilised (over time) positive attitude towards complying with any possible mechanism of production and distribution of any other good.

On the logic of the overall argument and on the substantive points, on the one hand, the book should speak for itself. On the other hand, the concerns that underlie the book may profit from some additional introductory notes. There are indeed several ways to read this book and move through it.

The main underlining concern of this book is to reemphasise the centrality of the vertical dimension of the political in an age in which a horizontal understanding prevails. As chapter 1 illustrates, an alternation of predominantly vertical and horizontal visions and conceptions of the political and of politics characterises Western political thought, and these conceptions naturally mirror and accompany specific historical experiences. In the decades since the end of World War II, a progressively more horizontal vision and understanding of the political have prevailed, to the point of largely obfuscating its vertical dimension. The terms 'politics' and 'political' have exploded to cover all sorts of newly developing horizontal phenomena and almost every type of human interaction. We now speak about politics in school councils, as well as in international meetings of heads of state; we admit the presence of politics in every specific and detailed policy; we see politics at work in student gatherings, in secret lobbying, in corporation management, in every kind of stakeholder negotiation, in the judiciary and in administrative bureaucracies. We regard as 'political' any collective action dilemma that stems from the coordination problems of independent individuals. Collective negotiations, deals and arrangements have expanded the realm of 'politics' in a colossal way. The formation of collective actors based on the free will of members has become an object of intense study, from social movements to interest groups to party systems. The study of individual participant behaviours, such as protest, pressure and voting, has expanded to a high level of sophistication. At the same time, international and regional integration and governance structures with no or tenuous binding implications have emphasised their 'political' dimension. What politics is about dilutes out to the infinite corners of our complexifying national and international environments.

From the local to the global, and from the single individual protester to top decision-makers, politics has been so much diluted that we may find any attempt to reflect on its specific nature daunting. The horizontal explosion of politics[1] has unquestionably fostered a relative neglect of its vertical dimension centred on decisions, possible coercion, violence and the imposition of outcomes, but what impresses more is the *mare magnum* of politics that we live in. In my view, this obfuscation of verticality is unhealthy from the knowledge point of view, and sometimes it presents itself as an ideological world of flattened and hyper-individualised entities.

The concern of this book is to see whether behind this phenomenological effervescence it is still possible to retrace the nucleus of the political in its archetypal form. I try to reemphasise the vertical dimension of the political in three ways. First, I advance an understanding of 'political action' as an inherently vertical interaction of incitation and response, of command and compliance. Second, I underline the inherent and unavoidable stratification of the political in relation to command and rule. Third, I put the accent on the crucial distinction between competition for 'who' rules and competition for 'what' is or will be done when ruling, where the former epitomises the most obvious verticality of politics and the latter its most obvious horizontality.

What I call the 'flattened' vision of politics – a vision of politics that forgets its verticality and stratification – manifests itself in many intellectual streams. One of the most evident instances is the redefinition of the political that takes place through the impact of economics on political science. Politics was connected with ethics in ancient Greek thinking, with God in the Christian ecclesia, with law in the formation of modern absolutist states and with society in the age of great social conflicts. Politics is increasingly connected with economics in the age of its domestication. I am not speaking against this strong new connection, nor do I want to underestimate its many important contributions. However, like any previous connection, this last one is not without its implications. From economic theories we often derive an overoptimistic view of the political in a dispassionate world of exchanges and contracts, free riding and cooperation problems and in a flattened landscape of independent and autonomous actors.[2] In the pacified, legalised, organisationally dense and cognitively mobilised Western environment, the language

---

1. For the thesis that any political experience emphasising the horizontal dimension of community participation and deliberation needs to refer to the conditions of the polis, see Miller, E.F. (1980), 'What Does "Political" Mean?', *The Review of Politics*, 42: 56–72, esp. pp. 63–65.

2. The description of politics as interaction among citizens 'characterised by a smooth conclave utility function defined over a basket of market-supplied goods and services . . . and a basket of government-provided goods and services' (Breton, Albert [1996], *Competitive Government. An Economic Theory of Politics and Public Finance*, Cambridge: Cambridge University Press, p. 38) is perhaps an exaggeratedly disfigured portrait. However, in its extremism this definition illustrates some of the linguistic problems I allude to.

of politics often changes inadvertently: from vertical command to horizontal negotiation, from government to governance, from conflict to obstacles to cooperation, from search for compliance to coordination games, from power of man over man to contracts. The sliding of the language reflects a change of cares. This risks delivering an elegantly fictitious 'science of politics' which is progressively uninterested and increasingly unaware of the fundamental predicaments that still lie behind even the most domesticated and pacified forms of the political. This book attempts to excavate and lay bare the foundations of the political order without focusing too much on the niceties of the surface building. Although the buildings differ enormously, and the differences make a difference to our lives, the means of grounding and the hidden underground foundations are more similar and more generalisable than is usually acknowledged.

Another flattening of the vision of politics occurs, again inadvertently, through a predominance of typically Western concerns and issues. Political science is the product of the pluralistic and polyarchic phases of political development, more than of any other different experience. Recently, however, we have gone too far, perhaps, in generalising these experiences and measuring everything else with their yardstick. There are normative, empirical and mundane good reasons for this. We regard this experience as desirable or at least more desirable than any other known. Most political scientists in the world are trained in this experience and in its universalisation. It is relatively easier to study the details of voting behaviour and the varieties of congressional committee life than to investigate the *arcana imperii* of the less open forms of the political. Sometimes, the methodological hyper-sophistication of the trivial offers better career opportunities. These biases are understandable and explainable in terms of the sociology of our profession, but they are unhealthy.

Let me conclude this introduction by mentioning a couple of other concerns that are less central but nevertheless present in the book. In most of my previous books, I have heavily focused on long-term historical dynamics. This book is of a different nature. It is largely analytical and betrays a preoccupation with theory of the archetypal forms of politics as a precondition for the analysis of its dynamic processes. With no doubt, the goal of political science research is to understand the sources, the mechanisms and the dynamics of political change. Nevertheless, a theoretical reconstruction of its archetypal forms is a prerequisite for any dynamic analysis to the extent that it precisely defines the 'objects' of the change processes we observe. Analytical discussions are often guilty of excessive abstraction and a lack of historical and empirical accuracy and completeness. However, the dynamics of change can hardly make up for this. A clear taxonomy and analytical discussion of the essential political forms must underline any programme of dynamic analysis.

This book, therefore, emphasises analytical and archetypal forms, leaving historical and empirical details in the background.

The book also witnesses an interest in the kind of general analytical framework that can give systemic significance to detailed empirical study. Recently, a variety of sub-sectoral and sub-disciplinary approaches have expanded, often with poor cross-linkages and without any comprehensive framework within which they can assume a more general significance. Today, our students rapidly enrol in these specialised subsectors and in particular methodological schools but often fail to relate their studies to the broader macro-questions of politics. This book considers contributions from different schools and attempts to offer a general framework within which the expanding variety of detailed and specialised empirical studies may acquire a broader meaning and relate more directly to the fundamental issues underlying the political.

Clearly, this book retraces my own understanding of the political as distilled from my work on it. At an advanced stage of a career of study mostly driven by substantive interests and concerns, a scholar is bound to reflect analytically on the nature of the object to which he has devoted energy and passion. Over a life of labour, a vision of the general topic progressively consolidates, and in this book I have tried to put order and coherence into this vision.

A last word about the broader project. What here takes the form of a small book was originally the first part of a broader enterprise. I aimed to proceed to an analysis of political actors, political institutions and political structures (stable and recurrent patterns of behaviours not institutionally prescribed) and to eventually move on to the dynamic aspects of the political process. There is no certainty that I will be able to complete the overall plan. As I said, the book should stand alone and speak for itself, but it should be understood that it was meant as a first stone and therefore inevitably sets aside some crucial aspects of the political.

Acknowledgements

I first sketched the core idea of this book in the keynote speech on the occasion of the fortieth anniversary of the Department of Political Science of the University of Geneva (2010, 'Politics as Confinement', in *Mélanges à l'occasion du 40e anniversaire du Département de Science politique*, sous la direction de William Ossipow, Genève: Université de Genève, pp. 29–42). An extended version has appeared in a volume of essays to honour the ninetieth anniversary of Giovanni Sartori (2015, 'Rivisitando 'Cosa è Politica' di Giovanni Sartori', in S. Passigli (ed.) *La Politica come Scienza. Scritti in onore di Giovanni Sartori*, Firenze: Passigli Editori, pp. 57–84).

My gratitude goes to the friends who have endured reading early versions of this book, offering suggestions and criticisms: Maurizio Ferrera, Adrienne Heritier, Hanspeter Kriesi, Leonardo Morlino and Joseph H.H. Weiler. I thank David Barnes for the English copy-editing of the manuscript.

Chapter 1

Trajectories of the political

The domain of human action that we conventionally define as 'politics' is plagued with events and shattered by personalities. Moreover, it is an inherently dangerous domain, as through it men can injure and rob, not to mention ruin themselves. The realm of the political engenders no teleological optimisms or invisible hands, and the vigour of wills breeds no harmonious combination or good outcome. Hands are visible in politics and are often armed. Unsurprisingly, the discussion of the concept of 'politics' has always evidenced a striking diversity of perspectives and approaches, and a definite lack of a common vocabulary or of a dominant view. Therefore, although the reflection is hardly new, the questions of what is political, what is specific about it and what should be the knowledge task of the political scientist have proven particularly difficult to address. Even a short review of previous investigations and responses would keep us busy for a long time, and there is no scope in this book to analyse this large body of thought in critical depth.

Understanding of the political evolves, of course, and in this introductory chapter I briefly focus on its main trajectories to pave the way for my own elaboration. First, predominantly 'vertical' or 'horizontal' conceptualisations have alternated in the history of visions of 'politics'. In the phases of horizontal predominance, politics spreads through all the interstices of the human experience, inextricably links to other dimensions of such experience and becomes ubiquitous and hard to grasp in its essential features. In the periods in which a vertical vision prevails, politics tends to be studied via characterisations that transcend its phenomenology, with definitions focusing on its essentialist nature and specific character.

Second, the vertical and horizontal conceptions of politics that have historically alternated have both been affected by a process of segmentation of the domains of human action in which politics has been progressively separated from other spheres of action, and the discipline of politics has been separated from the neighbouring disciplines of law, sociology, economics, theology, philosophy and so on.

Third, twentieth-century conceptions of politics continue to reflect the vertical and horizontal dimensions while engaging with a politics dismembered of its connections with other disciplines. Politics is connected with ethics in ancient Greek thinking, with God in the Christian ecclesia, with law in the formation of modern absolutist states and with society in the age of great social conflicts. It increasingly connects with economics in the age of its domestication.

HORIZONTAL AND VERTICAL CONCEPTIONS

We recognise the starting point of any conception of politics in the Greek term πολιτικος, *politicos*, presumably, but not certainly, having the same pre-Indo-European root as the term Πόλεμος, *polemos*, war. The famous Aristotelian definition of man as a 'political animal' (*zoon politikon*) was a definition of 'man', not of 'politics'. 'Politics' as such was undefined. In the Greek experience, a man's participation in the *polis* was not a part of his life but its essence. A 'non-political' man was a defective animal who had lost the plenitude of his fusion with and within the *polis*. The political intertwined so much with the human experience that it was undefinable as a separate sphere of life or activity. In fact, ancient Greek did not possess the word 'social' and did not distinguish political life from social life.[1]

In the Greek view, the *polis* was a particular and unprecedented way of managing internal affairs by virtue of one crucially innovative instrument: people talking one to one other as members of a collectivity of freemen and equals, sharing the duty and the right to constitute the *polis* and to generate and modify the specific arrangements to deal with its internal and external problems. This unprecedented innovation was verbally represented by the preamble introducing Greek laws that, as we have no systematic collection of Greek law, presumably started to be used in the seventh- or sixth-century BC: *edoxe te boule kei to demo*, 'it seems right to the council and to the people'. The striking modernity of the formula lies in its pragmatism (it seems right) and in its reference to the ultimate source

---

1. The best historical reviews of the lemma 'politics' include Sartori, Giovanni (1973), 'What Is "Politics"', *Political Theory*, 1: 5–26, originally published as Sartori, Giovanni (1972), 'La scienza politica', in Luigi Firpo (ed.) *Storia delle idee politiche, economiche e sociali*, Torino: UTET; Sellin, Volker (1978), 'Politik', in *Geschichtliche Grundbegriffe*, Band 4, Stuttgart: Klett-Cotta, pp. 789–874; and Ornaghi, Lorenzo (2013), 'Politica', in *Nell'età della tarda democrazia. Scritti sullo stato, le istituzioni e la politica*, Milano: Vita e Pensiero, pp. 65–73.

(the people).² People were supposed to voice their views, discuss those of others, try to persuade each other and eventually come to final decisions (often by voting). The same people were in principle eligible to be empowered, temporarily, to lead the others. This vision of the political process eventually led to decisions regarded as agreed upon by the collectivity, and which could therefore be imposed on it and associated with sanctioning non-compliers, be they opponents or opportunists, under the revolutionary implied concept of *isonomia*, the equality of citizens before the law.³

Isonomia and self-determination of the free were not, however, the foundation of the term 'democracy', which we now use in a positive sense. While the classical Greek intellectuals unanimously praised equality and freedom, they did not praise democracy. Democracy betrayed its social character of government by the 'poor' in their own interest, rather than the more recent meaning of government by the many or by the majority.⁴ In *Laws*, Plato complains that government by the many, by the populace and therefore inevitably by the poor is not subject to laws but superior to them and the final arbiter of them. From this comes the usual preference for mixed forms of government.

Notwithstanding the diffidence about government by the multitude (democracy), this conception of politics was distinctly horizontal. 'Politicalness' was not a vertical relationship between the 'governed' or 'ruled' and the 'government' or 'rulers' but mainly pertained to the relationships among citizens (although coercion was certainly not absent).⁵ The horizontal dimension and its participation practices were so important that the political experience was unviable beyond a certain number of free citizens. Its survival was unthinkable with the constitution of broader territorial and demographic units. However, it is surprising to note how much the legacy of this very particular and clearly 'unviable' (in different political units) conception has shaped the Western understanding of 'politics'. The revolutionary nature of this experience was so overwhelming that we have tended to universalise an idealised reconstruction of it through the political education of generations of intellectuals in the West.

---

2. A point is made in Castoriadis, Cornelius (1993; 1974), *Political and Social Writings, vol. 3 (1961–1979)*, Minneapolis and London: University of Minnesota Press, p. 164.

3. Poggi, G. (2014), *Varieties of Political Experiences. Power Phenomena in Modern Society*, Colchester: ECPR Press, pp. 1–2.

4. See Aristotle (350 BC; 2013, 2nd ed.), *Politics*, translated and with an introduction, notes and glossary by Carnes Lord, Chicago and London: University of Chicago Press, Books 3 and 4, pp. 62–128. For the consensus on this point among classical Greek thinkers, see the anthology of the most important writings on the form of government in Fassò, G. (1959), *La democrazia in Grecia*, Bologna: Il Mulino.

5. It is not that the Greek polis did not know or use 'coercion'; it is rather that coercion played no role in their understanding of the route to reaching collective decisions and was seen as a necessary tool only for punishing deviance from the properly achieved common standings.

This experience was not the only one and not the dominant one in the world before, during and after the *polis*. Beyond the Greek *polis*, small village communities, larger possessions of lords or even vaster empires managed such common goods and collective activities with completely different, if not opposite, understandings. The Greek thinking regarded none of these as 'political'. All those experiences that repressed and denied, or reserved, the practice of language and reason for the management of collective affairs to a few privileged individuals were indeed regarded as 'non-political'; a more 'vertical' dimension of the political dominated phases and realities unlike the small city and the constitution or reconstitution of large-scale political entities. It prevailed in successive Western and Eastern political experiences focusing on the empirically sharp differences that existed between rulers and subjects. This differentiation of roles resulted from a more marked differentiation and contrast of interests and from the corresponding idea that rulers have an interest in maintaining their subjects in a position of subordination and in denying them a possibility of self-determination and of defining and pursuing their own interests as separate from those of the rulers. The 'vertical' conception of politics emerges, therefore, from the profound asymmetries among different social components of a polity (of a larger size) and the struggle for power distribution following from these asymmetries of economic, ideological, symbolic or coercive resources. In this understanding, a part of society tends to define itself as the whole and to forget shared commitments to engage in compromise and mutual adjustment by imposing its own visions and interests.

Successive Western terminological innovations witnessed a continual tension between the horizontal and vertical dimensions. These remained influenced by the original Greek source but were found difficult to apply to the new realities on a different scale. The concepts derived from the word 'polis' shaped the understanding of successive horizontal experiences. If *politiké* indicated the art of government, *politeia* pointed to what we would today call the 'constitution' (or the 'regime'), the form of government and the techniques and organisation for the distribution of offices and charges in the city government. But the same term also included the definition of citizenship, of its obligations and duties and, furthermore, in an inextricable mix, the citizens as a whole, their 'togetherness', and also their education, the 'spirit' of the city, the essence of the *polis* and citizenship as an ethical way of life.[6] Therefore, Plato labels his work devoted to the living spirit, the ethos and definitely the essence of the *polis* as *politeia* – nowadays translated as 'republic' (*res publica*). Aristotle instead labels his treaty that deals with

---

6. See Bordes, J. (1982), *Politeia dans la pensée grecque jusqu'à Aristote*, Paris: Les Belles Lettres.

themes nearer to the modern positivist view of politics as study of the technical forms of government with a derivative term, *politikon* – now translated as 'politics' or 'the political'.

The word 'social' was a Latin invention, although the medieval translators of Aristotle ended up attributing it to him. Latin thinking and language used *civis* and *civitas* for what the Greek labelled *polites*.[7] However, *civitas* had lost most of the political connotation of the Greek *politis* as it was organised juridically in a *juris societas*. The Romans used the term *res publica* for what we could identify as 'politics'. However, a 'vertical' dimension was also absent from this terminology.[8]

The original Greek terms disappeared for almost ten centuries until the rediscovery of the Aristotelian works in the thirteenth century. When these works were directly translated into Latin from Greek (in approximately 1260), the term 'politics' made a new entry on the scene. William of Moerbeke (1215), a Flemish Dominican, used a 'Greekish' version of the term, *politikos*, for which he was to be accused of monkish literalness. He might have chosen this literal translation out of uncertainty about the real meaning of the original term and therefore found it preferable to leave it 'Greekish'. Perhaps modern languages acquired the lemma thanks to this insecurity about translation.[9] St. Thomas Aquinas (1225) simply translated the term as 'politics'. In the Middle Ages, the art of ruling and government persisted as part of the definition of politics, but there was nothing that resembled the idea of *politeia*, perhaps because there was nothing that resembled the specific territoriality of the Greek *polis*. Quite the contrary, one could say that in the ideals and praxis of medieval politics there was something alien and even hostile about the Greek concept of *politeia*. Christianity, the new element of togetherness, presented itself as hostile to politics on grounds of principle, as it was identified with the world of power, violence, abuse and temptation. The connection between ethics and politics was the opposite to the Greek one. Politics was not a source of ethical behaviour and the sphere of ethical action but rather its contrary. The Christian and medieval thinking (from St. Augustine) located ethics definitely outside politics, which was seen as something inevitably corrupt. Even medieval law presented itself as a law without politics. It was more an expression of society than of the state and manifested itself in traditions and orders that coexisted. They maintained themselves thanks to the inability of political power to unify and standardise

---

7. For the distinction between *civitas* and *urbs* in the Roman experience, see Foustel de Coulanges, Numa Denis (1956; 1980), *The Ancient City. A Study of Religion, Laws and Institutions of Greece and Rome*, Baltimore: Johns Hopkins University Press, pp. 126–34.

8. Sartori, 'What Is "Politics"', p. 9.

9. Sternberger, Dolf (1982), ' "Politics" in Language. Twelve Notes on the History of Words and Meanings', in M. Cranston and P. Mair (eds.), *Language and Politics*, Bruxelles: Bruylant, p. 27.

all social manifestations because of its incapacity to extend itself to all areas of intersubjective relations, therefore allowing for wide areas of interference by competing powers.[10]

This was only the first of a complex series of linguistic and conceptual re-elaborations of the original *polis/politikon* terms that progressively represented the different political experiences of the Western world. The Middle Ages more explicitly conceptualised the vertical dimension in the political process by resorting to new and different concepts, such as *dominium*, *princeps* and *principatum*. Politics inevitably began to be more explicitly associated with this vertical dimension.

Unsurprisingly, the horizontal dimension of politics, which was absent from the concepts of politics and government in the Middle Ages, re-emerged forcefully in the thinking of the Renaissance city-states, having been rediscovered through the mediation of the Roman Republic and its 'public law'. Undoubtedly, Machiavelli's concept of *virtù* represents a form of heathen ideal that reproduces the Greek ideal of politics as ethics. However, a new alternation in the dominant ideal occurred with the demise of the Renaissance city-states before the growing influence of the new, modern, large territorial states. In the same vein in which the pre-modern conceptions of politics in the period 800–1300 had to refer to the Christian community and ecclesia, since the sixteenth-century discourse about politics has carried an ever-closer connection with the concept of the state, with constant association and reference to it. The new entity that consolidated through the seventeenth and eighteenth centuries progressively monopolised political discourse. The development of the state allowed the redefinition of politics that, albeit differently, both Hobbes and Machiavelli operated. The concepts of ruling and being ruled, rulers and the ruled, obligations, laws and so forth were redefined in reference to the state. The modern-age and the post-Westphalian state-making process allowed a predominant vertical dimension of politics to re-emerge, strongly connected to the form of the bureaucratic and military state, which would only be challenged by the liberalisation and democratisation processes of the nineteenth and twentieth centuries.

After a long period in which the vertical dimension was predominant, in the contemporary age, politics has again been rebalanced with a growing horizontal dimension. The study of what we call contemporary politics focuses on collective action problems, participation practices, decentralisation mechanisms, social movements, stakeholder involvement in authoritative decisions, governance and so forth – all concepts that refer to a newly reaffirmed horizontal dimension of politics. On the one hand, this re-emergence of the horizontal

---

10. See Grossi, Paolo (1997), *L'ordine giuridico medioevale*, Roma-Bari: Laterza, pp. 41–49.

dimension generates new pushes for localism and small-scale communities in search of the ideal size in which the community dimension of politics can recover. On the other hand, it paradoxically goes together with an ever-growing centralisation of resources and decision-making power in large corporate actors.

It is perhaps not fully accurate, but it is definitely tempting, to relate the purely vertical and horizontal conceptions of politics to the two great antagonists, Hobbes and Rousseau. Rousseau's scheme of extreme and pure democracy stands in sharp contrast to Hobbes's defence of pure political authority. Both, however, intended to prevent any emergence of other political forces in the polity and shared a profound dislike for any sort of intermediate authority formation above the atomised citizens as coequals – for Rousseau – or below the monistic sovereign – for Hobbes. Both would certainly regard the organised, mobilised, fragmented politics of our polyarchies as evil for their respective and definitely opposed ideal polities. Neither the extreme puritan democracy of Rousseau nor the absolutist authority of Hobbes see any place for competing and conflicting associations, and the political clashes of our contemporary politics were alien to both.

THE DISMEMBERING OF POLITICS

In parallel with, and somewhat independently of, the alternation of emphasis between the vertical and horizontal conceptions of the political, we observe a progressive fragmentation of the understanding of the human experience of which politics is a part. The early 'integrated' political experience has been progressively 'dismembered', fragmented into a set of separate subfields of activity, each with its own rules and legitimising principles.

Machiavelli and Hobbes are the founders of the separation of politics and its study from any consideration and reasoning of an ethical or religious nature. In laying the foundation for the autonomy of the political they ended the tradition that from St. Augustine's (350–430) *De Civitate Dei* to St. Thomas's (1225–1274) *Summa Theologiae* despised the world of politics for a thousand years while trying to firmly ground it in the 'holiness of law', whether it was 'eternal', 'goodly', 'natural' or 'human' law. The philosophical and deductive style of Hobbes's thinking led him to an extremised vision in which the political is not only autonomous and independent but is also all-including: the Leviathan creates and determines everything else. Machiavelli, with the empirical eyes of a more disenchanted observer, simply aimed to discover the rules that a prince had to use if he wanted to be successful. Terminologically, the term 'politics' would be used again by Althusius (1603), Spinoza (1677) and Bossuet (1670), but the definition of what politics is was becoming progressively more complex.

The development and differentiation of the specialised machinery of the large territorial state and the prevailing association of politics with its hierarchy and activities produced a further differentiation of the sphere of politics. A major step in the separation of the understanding of 'politics' from that of other realms of life came with the rebirth of the old Roman concept of *civitas*, society, and its new claim to independence and an a priori existence with respect to politics (the antithetical position to that of Hobbes). The differentiation between 'society' and 'politics' took place slowly from the Renaissance onwards. It took its final form with natural law thinking, the contractualist tradition and the emergence of the new idea of a 'contract' between a sovereign and the subjects as a way to fill the vertical gap, at least in part.

If secularisation had tended to reduce the concern of politics with matters of faith and relationships with ecclesiastical authorities, marketisation tended to reduce the involvement of politics in economic affairs. The idea insinuated itself that matters concerning the production and distribution of wealth should be better left to the activities of profit-seeking individuals. The limitations set on politics by secularisation and marketisation corresponded with each other and fostered the development of a new sphere of equal and free individuals in the space progressively identified as 'civil society',[11] which was similar to the Greek *polis* relationships among free and equal individuals but without the political dimension of collective decision-making that typified it.

Locke, Montesquieu and the liberal constitutionalists saw society as composed of pre-existing bodies and orders whose autonomy had to be preserved. Even Hegel forcefully maintained the distinction between state and civil society in his *Philosophy of Right* (1820/1821). Civil society was the realm where individuals engage in the pursuit of their private interests, and the tensions with the 'state' that this dualism generated were moderated, in his view, by the presence of intermediate institutions such as the family, the corporation and public administration – all distinctly 'non-political' institutions.[12] A most radical and crucial differentiation of economic life from political authority had been asserted by Adam Smith, Ricardo and, more generally, the laissez-faire thinkers. They emphasised the view that social life finds its own principle of self-organisation and can prosper if, and only if, it is left alone without interference from other spheres of life and, above all, without 'political' interference. This new thinking would see the autonomy of society

---

11. On the state–civil society relationship, see the classic work by von Humbolt written in 1792 and published in 1851: von Humbolt, W. (1969), *The Limits of State Action*, Cambridge: Cambridge University Press. For a comprehensive anthology, see also Pellzynski, Z.A. (ed.) (1984), *The State and Civil Society*, Cambridge: Cambridge University Press.

12. See Riedel, M. (1984), ' "State" and "Civil Society": Linguistic Context and Historical Origin', in *Between Tradition and Revolution: The Hegelian Transformation of Political Philosophy*, Cambridge: Cambridge University Press.

specifically in the sphere of individual economic transactions and contracts. The new independent status of 'society' was certified by its becoming the object of new sciences, one that Comte (1798–1857) was to label 'sociology' and another that Smith and Ricardo would denote as 'political economy', well before 'economics' was suggested as a shorter term for economy and science in the late nineteenth century. Somewhat paradoxically, civil society was seen as free and equal in the management of its own private dealings and activities exactly in the age in which new ideas supported a progressive widening of the state's spheres of legitimate activities and a will to regulate, control or coerce levies on stocks and flows of private wealth, or through public debt. All this was carried out by an expanding body of public employees.

In passing, it is interesting to note that the scholars who have recently relaunched the 'civil society' concept and analysis of it have explicitly excluded economic activities and institutions from it, thus identifying the three separate domains of 'politics' (the state), 'the market' and 'civil society'. The last of these is seen as the place for the development of collective identities, solidarities, non-market– or non-profit–oriented interactions and social movements, and so on – the 'third sector'.[13]

Finally, the liaison between politics and the law was also broken when the political system came to no longer be seen as primarily a juridical system. The relative separation of law and politics was the result of intense efforts on both sides. On the one hand, the predominance of the set of legal theories going under the label of 'legal positivism' and the 'pure theory of law' represented a forceful professionalisation of legal studies. These theories provided a way to approach the study of law from a factual point of view or as a technical expression of sovereignty or as an identification of justice with law.[14] In any case, the separation from the realm of production of law (by the sovereign) was accentuated. On the other hand, particularly in the United States at the end of the nineteenth century, a growing critique of the excessive 'legalism' of traditional political studies led to the sparking of the behavioural 'revolution', which in redefining 'institutions' as behavioural regularities definitely sharpened the distance between the two spheres and disciplines.[15] When the strong historical correspondence between state/law and politics dissolved and political processes began to expand beyond the field of the state and its institutions, politics somehow lost any element of institutional identification.

---

13. Such as in Cohen, Jean and Andrew Arata (1992), *Civil Society and Political Theory*, Cambridge, MA: MIT Press.
14. For these three readings of legal positivism, see Bobbio, Norberto (1965), *Giusnaturalismo e positivismo giuridico*, Bari: Laterza.
15. Dahl, A. Robert (1961), 'The Behavioural Approach in Political Science: Epitaph for a Monument to a Successful Protest', *American Political Science Review* 55: 763–73.

In line with these tendencies, the political philosophy of the twentieth century moved towards a definition of the political somewhat detached from the classical reference to the state and the rulership stratification that it represented. Philosophical attempts to define the political resorted less frequently to the law/state connection as a privileged background. Sometimes, more encompassing and anodyne terms such as 'political system' or 'political community' substituted the term 'state'.[16] In other cases, the connection with law/state definitively disappears. Major scholars such as Dunn, Arendt, Oakeshott, Collingwood and Strauss defined politics as something different from the ruler-ruled relationships in the statist tradition.[17] Even Schmitt and de Jouvenel strove to define politics without reference to the state. Schmitt's *amicus-nemicus* category is clearly prior to any institutional definition referring to rulership. De Jouvenel's elementary political action (to which I will come back extensively later) similarly takes the lead from a particular kind of interpersonal relationship.[18]

In recent times, the emphasis on the opposition between the horizontal (community) and the vertical (coercion) terminology and conception of the political has attenuated. At least in the Westernised politics of the democratic age, the horizontal dimension, so typical of city-state republican experiences, and the vertical dimension, so dominant in the period of the formation of states and empires, are now inexorably mixed. At the same time, progressively 'denuded' of or 'dismembered'[19] from ethics, religion, economy, society and law, politics has become different and autonomous and is left alone. The study of politics is more 'ubiquitous', both horizontally and vertically,[20]

---

16. See the critique in Finer, S.E. (1969–1970), 'Almond's Concept of "The Political System": A Textual Critique', *Government and Opposition*, V: 3–21.

17. Typical examples are Dunn, John (2000), *Cunning of the Unreason: Making Sense of Politics*, London: HarperCollins; Arendt, H. (1958), *The Human Condition*, Chicago: Chicago University Press; Oakeshott, M. (1975), *On Human Conduct*, Oxford: Clarendon Press; Collingwood, R.G. (1943), *The New Leviathan*, Oxford: Clarendon Press; Strauss, L. (1959), *What Is Political Philosophy?*, Glencoe, IL: The Free Press.

18. De Jouvenel, Bertrand (1954; 1992), 'The Nature of Politics', in Dennis Hale and Marc Landy (eds.), *The Nature of Politics: Selected Essays of Bertrand de Jouvenel*, New Brunswick, NJ: Transaction, pp. 67–83; Schmitt, Carl (1927; 1966), *The Concept of the Political*, translated by George Schwab, Chicago: University of Chicago Press, pp. 27–37; or Schmitt, Carl (ed.) (1927), 'Der Begriff des Politischen', *Archiv für Sozialwissenschaften und Sozialpolitik*, 58: 1–33. The same applies to the more esoteric approaches of Rancière, J. (1999), *Disagreement: Politics and Philosophy*, Minneapolis: University of Minneapolis Press; Alexander, J. (2014), 'Notes towards a Definition of Politics', *Philosophy*, 89: 273–300; Badiou, A. (1998), *Abrégé de métapolitique*, Paris: Editions du Seuil; Mouffe, Chantal (2005), *On the Political*, London: Routledge.

19. 'Denuded' is the term used in Sartori's 'What Is "Politics"' to describe this process. Palonen uses 'dismembered' very much in the same vein in Palonen, Kari (2006), 'Two Concepts of Politics: Conceptual History and Present Controversies', *Scandinavian Journal of Social Theory*, 7: 11–25, esp. pp. 11–12.

20. On the modern ubiquity of power (politics), see Popitz, H. (1992, 2nd ed.), *Phaenomene der Macht*, Tübingen: J.C.B. Mohr. An English translation of the first chapter of this very important work is available in Poggi, G. (2014), *Varieties of Political Experiences*, pp. 163–65.

more 'autonomous', in the sense of standing alone, and more 'professionalised', in terms of the number of its practitioners, specialised reviews, topics, fields and subfields, approaches, schools and sects.[21] An autonomous and dismembered 'politics' has been fragmented and redefined as 'political system', 'political communication', 'political participation', 'political socialisation', 'political development', 'public policy' and 'political economy' and so forth in a multiplication of subfields in which the adjective 'political' becomes an addendum of relatively soft theoretical significance to the substantive concern, be it development, economy, policies, communication or any other field. Along this line, the political is more difficult to define in its special character. Often it has been hetero-defined, that is, defined by those spheres that have historically separated from it: the sociology of politics, the economics of politics, the ethics of politics and so on. Recent conceptions of this 'denuded' politics witness these difficulties.

CONCEPTIONS OF 'DISMEMBERED' POLITICS

With the same speed and inevitable simplification with which I have reviewed political terminology from Greek antiquity to modern times, I now move on to reviewing the main contributions of the twentieth century to the definition of 'politics', regrouping them into six main families.[22] The focus of the review is on the main approaches to the problem. Scholars and schools are characterised by their main theme, while they often resort to more complex and composite criteria. This reconstruction does not review critically and thoroughly the thought of single prominent scholars. Instead, through reference to them it characterises the main directions along which the attempt to define the political travels.

Politics as activities

A first line of thought engages in defining politics through the activities that common-sense perceptions attribute to it. A discussion on the nature of the

---

21. Almond, A. Gabriel (1988), 'Separate Tables: Schools and Sects in Political Science', *PS: Political Science and Politics*, 21: 828–42.

22. I was tempted to add a seventh 'family', making reference to a conception of politics as a practice, and in particular as a linguistic practice. The emphasis of much of twentieth-century philosophy on language as a constitutive property of the human experience and as the ontological reality of the political would justify this. The work of scholars such as Russell, Saussure, Husserl, Wittgenstein, Lacan, Derrida and Foucault includes elements of such a vision. However, I have been unable to systematise these somewhat-scattered elements of a conception of politics as language into a relatively coherent paradigm. See Cranston, Maurice (1982), 'The Language of Politics', in M. Cranston and P. Mair (eds.), *Language and Politics*, pp. 11–24.

political is not mandatory if we believe we know what constitutes politics and what politics is about. As Maurice Cranston put it in his usual straightforward language, ' "Politics" is a world which seems to me to need no definition. We all know how to use it, and we are liable to be confused only if we rely on definitions provided by political scientists'.[23] However, even an emphasis on politics as 'acting' or on politics as a 'practice' does not seem to produce the obvious meaning Cranston alludes to if we consider that Plato compared acting politicians to flute players, Oakeshott concluded that politics as a practice could be compared to the art of cookery[24] and Cranston himself wondered whether politics should be regarded as a performing or a creative art.

Of course, distinctive *activities* may define politics: voting, legislative life, party propaganda, trade union–employer negotiations, legislation and so on. In other words, we may resort to a taxonomic approach to the definition of politics and political behaviours, listing those behaviours that intuitively belong to a class (political versus non-political), very much as lawyers define behaviours as lawful or unlawful. The tendency to identify politics with specific activities is a clear indication that in this domain the praxeological element and the reality of political life prevail over any shared theorising. This involves a definitive abandonment of any attempt to define the specificity of the political in general terms and to derive from it a conceptual guide to what is politically relevant or irrelevant. Moreover, this line of thought must accept a potential exponential growth of activities that a large community may eventually regard as 'politically relevant'.

One often attempts to define politics via a lexicographic formulation large enough to cover the endless list of phenomena that are intuitively political. Assuming one knows what all the instances of politics are, one can find a definition that includes them all. Along this line, discussions often focus on examples used to support or discard certain views of politics. A variety of definitions of politics can rapidly be refuted by making reference to activities, phenomena and events that are regarded as 'clear instances of politics', 'unquestionably belonging to politics' or 'an example of politics', and which are not included in the definition to be refuted.[25]

There is an inbuilt circularity in any attempt to define politics in a way that encompasses all its relevant instances. These require a definition of the political that cannot be left to mere intuition or common sense. Moreover, attempts to be inclusive lead to all-encompassing definitions. Accommodating the

---

23. Cranston, Maurice (1982), 'The Language of Politics', in M. Cranston and P. Mair (eds.), *Language and Politics*, Bruxelles: Bruylant, p. 11.
24. Oakeshott, Michael (1962), *Rationalism in Politics*, London: Methuen, p. 119.
25. These quotations are from one of the most extensive exercises of this type: Donahue, T.J. (2014), *What Is Politics?* Working Paper, 14 October.

variety of intuitive political manifestations stretches the concept of politics to a rarefied abstractness, which is only satisfactory because its terms are vague and ambiguous enough to include almost everything. The attempt to define the political in its supposed phenomenological entirety may lead to triviality or, worse, to the destruction of any specificity.

The 'deep ecology' school is the most all-encompassing attempt to characterise politics. It equates politics with human activities and choices, leaving little room for anything to be non-political. In this perspective, politics extends beyond human interactions, includes any activity which deserves ethical consideration by human beings and therefore also encompasses the relationship between human beings, even isolated ones, with inanimate or non-human animate beings in the natural environment.[26] Examples of such all-encompassing definitions abound: 'politics comprises all the activities of co-operation and conflict, within and between societies, whereby the human species goes about organising the use, production and distribution of human, natural and other resources in the production and reproduction of its biological and social life';[27] politics is an activity with two faces: (1) making, breaking and preserving the general arrangement of a group's affairs; (2) trying to get a group to take certain decisions when some members of the group oppose them.[28] These characterisations can easily accommodate almost everything, with no eventual advantage. The concept of politics is so 'stretched' that the certainty of not missing anything results in the certainty of defining nothing.

Defining politics by distilling an encompassing definition able to include a known list of activities is not a very interesting exercise.[29] In fact, however, this is most often the strategy in general labelling definitions at the beginning of textbooks on politics. We need to at least begin to identify some criteria from which to draw the political element of the set of facts, behaviours and activities that we conventionally regard as political.

Politics as institutional locus

Instead of defining politics via specific activities, one can search for a definition that is 'locational', that is, a definition that defines as political the

---

26. There could hardly be a broader vision of politics. Politics identifies with the presence of a duty towards something else. Inanimates and non-human animates are attributed rights and interests (supposedly defined by somebody else) and generate duties towards nature. See Burns, Tony (2000), 'What Is Politics? Robinson Crusoe, Deep Ecology and Immanuel Kant', *Politics*, 20: 93–98.
27. Leftwich, A. (1984), 'Politics: People, Resources and Power', in A. Leftwich (ed.), *What Is Politics?*, Oxford: Basic Blackwell, pp. 64–65.
28. Donahue, *What Is Politics?*
29. Frohock formulates an explicit critique of the taxonomic approach to the definition of politics. Frohock, F.M. (1978), 'The Structure of Politics', *American Political Science Review*, 72: 859–70, particularly pp. 865–67.

activities and behaviours that take place in specific institutional places that are 'political'. A spatial understanding of politics – as we may call it – requires a physical location, a 'locus'. This is most often identified in the 'state' or in slightly more abstract spaces such as 'political formations' (*politischer Verband*, Weber), 'political entities' (*politische Einheit*, Carl Schmitt), 'political communities' or even 'government'. The most clearly 'spatial' connotation of politics and that most referred to in textbooks is Easton's reference to politics as the inputs, outputs and processes of the 'political system'.

This is also the line followed by Sartori, who explicitly denies the possibility of defining politics or political action in any essentialist way: 'Political behaviour should not be understood literally. The expression does not point to any particular type of behaviour; rather it denotes a locus, a *site* of behaviour'.[30] The spatial metaphor in locational definitions refers to lines of demarcation or to more abstract divisions of spheres and immediately calls into question the idea of boundaries between politics and other types of activities or relations (which are not political).[31] Sartori solves the difficulty generated by moving the definition of politics from its intrinsic characteristics to its spatial location by pushing its reasoning to extreme consequences. In his view, any kind of activity or behaviour, the political as well as the social or economic, can be defined only in locational terms, in terms of the structures and roles in which it manifests itself. In his opinion, only the category of ethical behaviour escapes a spatial characterisation, that is, a definition of it as 'behaviour in . . . '.[32]

A spatial metaphor for the definition of the political leaves open the problem that it includes the terms to be defined in its own definition. Whatever place, institution, role or other entity we identify as the 'locus' of political activities or behaviours, its constitution remains mysteriously outside the realm of politics. It has to be treated as a 'given'. We end up giving away what constitutes, maintains or changes such spaces that identify the political. We exclude from politics its most fundamental and problematic component: the creation, modification and destruction of political communities, systems, institutions and so forth. Such ways of defining the 'political' have the advantage of cutting short the unpleasant definitional quarrel, but they do not have much else to recommend them.

---

30. Sartori, 'What Is "Politics"', p. 17.
31. Palonen, Kari (2006), 'Two Concepts of Politics: Conceptual History and Present Controversies', *Scandinavian Journal of Social Theory*, 7: 11–25. Palonen refers to two different concepts of politics: the 'sphere' and the 'activity' concepts.
32. Sartori, 'What Is "Politics"', p. 18. Note that Sartori, while underlining the historicity of the various conceptions of politics, does not adhere to the radical position of Nietzsche, according to whom it is possible to 'define' only inanimate entities, while concepts that have a historical development defy any definitional attempt.

Facing this problem, Sartori moves towards a more substantive definition of specific political activity. Political decisions binding erga omnes can be defined as 'sovereign' collectivised decisions from which it is most difficult to subtract, because of both their territorial and their coercive intensity. He nevertheless immediately underlines afterwards that 'if all these decisions are prejudicially "political" it is for the fact that they are taken by personnel located in political seats. This is their "political" nature'.[33] We will come back to these substantive definitional criteria at length later. For the moment, it seems that no locational criteria can get away without the most substantive definitional attributes.

Politics as conflict

A further conception of politics identifies its distinctive feature in the idea of conflicts among interests and conciliation of them. In this tradition, the essential aspect of politics is conflict among individuals, and a situation or phenomenon is political to the extent that it involves a conflict of interest, preferences and so on. This vision of politics as conflict and accommodation of interests dominated general theories of politics in the United States in the twentieth century.[34] Two concise definitions are (1) 'Genuinely political situations involve multiple and conflicting demands addressed to the same resources and occurring within the same institutional framework'[35] and (2) 'At a minimum politics has to do with the distribution of scarce and sought-after resources among contending parties'.[36] Politics is defined as that activity by which differing interests within a given unit of rule are reconciled by giving them a share of power in proportion to their importance to the welfare and survival of the whole community.[37] Conflict and antagonism are also at the core of the definition offered by Chantal Mouffe.[38] Warren suggests that politics is that subset of social relations characterised by conflict over goods in the face of pressure to associate for collective action, where at least one party to the conflict seeks collectively binding decisions and seeks

---

33. Sartori, 'What Is "Politics"', p. 21.
34. I leave aside here conflict theories of a more sociological nature, such as those of Marx, Coser and Dahrendorf. The entire works of Marx are permeated by social conflict and the prospects for overcoming it. Coser, Lewis (1956), *The Function of Social Conflict*, New York: The Free Press; Dahrendorf, Ralf (1959), *Class and Class Conflict in Industrial Society*, Stanford, CA: Stanford University Press. There is usually little 'politics' in them as the 'coalition' side is decidedly less developed.
35. Leftwich, *Politics: People, Resources and Power*, 39.
36. Bennett, W. Lance (1975), 'Political Scenarios and the Nature of Politics', *Philosophy and Rhetoric* 8: 23–42, esp. p. 26.
37. Crick, Bernard (1992), *In Defence of Politics*, London: Weidenfeld and Nicholson, p. 21.
38. Mouffe, Chantal (2005), *On the Political*, London: Routledge, p. 9.

to sanction decisions by means of power.³⁹ More clearly than those of the previous authors, in this last definition conflict is associated with power as a means to solve it, which justifies considering Warren among the scholars who emphasise power in their definition of politics (see next section). In Warren's view, conflict may exist without power being exercised, which defines situations that are non-political, and power may exist without any conflict being expressed, which he also defines as non-political to the extent that politics is 'suppressed' by exorbitant power.

This tradition sees politics as the arena in which interests enter, are dealt with through various processes and are finally transformed into outputs or policies, with or without feedback effects. Politics is confrontation and occasional struggle among individual or collective actors/agents who pursue different desires and interests in public matters, and its main function is to reconcile the diversity of individuals and their interests. Politics is an interaction of interests, desires and demands and how this interaction generates those structures that we call political.⁴⁰

It is debatable whether one can enrol Carl Schmitt within this family. Schmitt tries to define the core element of politics by making reference to contrast or conflict, but such conflicts assume *only* their 'political' character when their degree of 'intensity' is such as to generate an opposition between *amicus* and *nemicus*. Politics is the intensity that opposes us as enemies and friends. The intensity of the *amicus/nemicus* dichotomy finds its behavioural criteria in the possibility of violent conflict and in the possibility of the solution of the political problem via the physical annihilation of the *nemicus*. In this sense, politics finds its specific source in conflict, but the 'politicalness' of such conflicts rests in their potentially irreconcilable nature and the ever-present possibility of violent confrontation. Schmitt presents the undomesticated and non-domesticable side of the political and an extreme conception of politics which is characterised by the possibility of resorting to specific unpleasant and ultimate means.⁴¹ As such, his view also defines politics by its (extreme) means.

Politics as specific 'means': Power, coercion

A further line of thought about politics, perhaps the most familiar one, identifies politics with the typical means to which it resorts, usually power and

---

39. Warren, Mark E. (1999), 'What Is Political?', *Journal of Theoretical Politics*, 11: 207–31, esp. p. 218.
40. For a review of the post–World War II (WWII) 'politics of interest' literature, see Cochran, Clarke E. (1973), 'The Politics of Interests: Philosophy and the Limitations of the Science of Politics', *American Journal of Political Science*, 17: 745–66.
41. Schmitt, Carl (1996), *The Concept of the Political*.

coercion (or sheer violence, as in Schmitt, mentioned earlier). Whatever politics can be or does, its specificity lies in the resort to means that are particular to it.

Max Weber devoted many pages of his monumental work to power and its various forms, and he provided possibly the most extended definition of the concept as 'the chance of a man or a group of men to realise their own will in a social action even against the resistance of others who are participating in the action'.[42] Although coercion – legitimate or otherwise – is a crucial presence in all his writings, it is neither the explicative nor the definitional element of politics. Although politics may have a special relationship with violence as its extreme form, violence is not the substance of politics. Note that Weber used the monopoly of legitimate violence to define the essence of the modern state, not the essence of politics.[43] He rarely embarked on an explicit characterisation of 'politics' through power. In fact, Weber does not embark on any characterisation of 'politics' at all in *Economy and Society*. To the best of my knowledge, this happens only once, when he succinctly states without much elaboration that 'We define therefore politics as the aspiration to power or to an influence over the distribution of power, both among states and within one state, among the groups of people that it includes'.[44]

An explicit connection and identification of politics with power is notably the approach most clearly represented by authors such as George E. G. Catlin,[45] Harold D. Lasswell,[46] de Jouvenel,[47] Robert Dahl[48] and many other scholars following in the footsteps of this tradition.[49] It is unfair to enrol them all in one specific school as these significant authors have sophisticated

---

42. Weber, Max (1922; 1978), *Economy and Society*, Berkeley: University of California Press, p. 926.
43. See Poggi, G. (2014), *Varieties of Political Experiences*, p. 17.
44. This explicit but concise connection between power and politics reappears in Weber, M. (1991), 'Politics as a Vocation', in H. H. Gerth and C. Wright Mills (eds.), *From Max Weber: Essays in Sociology*, London: Routledge, p. 78.
45. Catlin holds that politics is the relations among men in so far as they seek to have their way with their fellows; Catlin, G. E. G. (1964), *The Science and Method of Politics*, Hamden, CT: Archon, pp. 210–11.
46. Lasswell, H. D. and A. Kaplan (1950), *Power and Society: A Framework for Political Inquiry*, New Haven, CT: Yale University Press.
47. See de Jouvenel, Bertrand (1963), *The Pure Theory of Politics*, Cambridge: Cambridge University Press.
48. Dahl sees politics as 'any persistent pattern of human relationship that involves, to a significant extent, control, influence, power or authority'; Dahl, R. (1963), *Modern Political Analysis*, Englewood Cliffs, NJ: Prentice Hall, pp. 8–9.
49. The list is definitely too long to be exhaustively cited. Masters defines politics as behaviour that simultaneously partakes of the attributes of bonding, dominance and submission and of the legal and customary regulation of social life; Masters, Roger D. (1989), *The Nature of Politics*, New Haven, CT: Yale University Press, p. 140. Wolff sees politics as 'the exercise of the power of the state, or the attempt to influence that exercise'; Wolff, R. P. (1970), *In Defence of Anarchism*, New York: Harper and Row, p. 4.

visions of the political process that deserve much scrutiny. However, it is correct to say that they all share an attribution of a central role to power, power fights and power aspirations in their conceptions of the political.

At least since *Power and Society* (1950), Lasswell has definitely identified 'politics' with 'power'. To the extent that it is characterised and influenced by power, the entire social process is 'political'. In this sense, there is no difference between the power of government, on the one hand, and any other form of power, on the other. Whatever power relation, wherever it manifests itself, it indicates and identifies a political relationship.[50] For Lasswell, where there is power there is ipso facto politics. In this case, any activity, phenomenon or relationship that is structured by power is political.

Another scholar of the twentieth century regarded power as an essentialist category of the political. Bertrand de Jouvenel offered a concise definition of politics as 'to make somebody else act' (according to your will, of course). De Jouvenel identified elementary political action in the movement of men by another man: 'I hold the view that we should regard as "political" every systematic effort, performed at any place in the social field, to move other men in pursuit of some design cherished by the mover'.[51] Very much in line with Lasswell, de Jouvenel therefore does not distinguish between power in general and power in a political context.[52] Their positions had the deliberate aim of separating the definition of the political from the structure and activities of government (the state, etc.), that is, from any locational characterisation.

This approach was criticised for its inability to identify the specific form of power that is inherently 'political'. Under the category of 'politics' these authors subsume any form of compliance due to a power relationship. The claim that the existence of a power structure makes a relationship political – whether it is master-slave, officer-private, male-female and so on – makes 'politics' indistinguishable from the many aspects of social life that involve power relationships, or, alternatively, redefines them as political in nature. The explosion of the political along this line is best epitomised by the feminist slogan 'the personal is political'. However, power – so the criticism runs – indicates a social relationship that is too general and pervasive to be

---

50. There is no space and in fact no need here to enter a more detailed discussion of the complex relation between the concept of power and that of 'influence' in Lasswell's work. The interested reader may refer to Zimmerling, Ruth (2006), *Influence and Power: Variations on a Messy Theme*, Dordrecht: Springer, chapter 2.

51. De Jouvenel, *The Pure Theory of Politics*, p. 30.

52. However, de Jouvenel's position is more sophisticated than Lasswell's assimilation of power with politics. He uses power to qualify 'elementary political action', not politics as such. Therefore, he defends his stand better from the usual accusation that the definition of the political in terms of power is excessively general. On this point, see Harbold, William H. (1953), 'Bertrand de Jouvenel on the Essence of Politics', *The Western Political Quarterly*, 6: 742–49; and Stoppino, M. (2001, 3rd ed.), *Potere e teoria politica*, Milano: Giuffré, pp. 213–216.

able to offer a theoretical object for the study of politics. Faced with this criticism, Lasswell and de Jouvenel replied that their vision challenged the conventional definition of politics centred on the concepts and the activities of government and the state. The new definition, centred on the reality of power, redefined politics in an unconventional and extensive way.

Scholars who have not found this line of argument satisfactory have focused on the possibility of specifying the nature of 'political power' with respect to other forms of power. Eckstein suggests that there is politics whenever there is a structure of authority, of whatever kind: a form of government, public or private.[53] Warren attempts to criticise the coextensive nature of politics with 'power' – and of politics with 'conflict' – as, in his view, politics 'encompasses a narrower range of social relations than do all power relations and all conflict relations'. His definition of politics combines power with conflict. Politics is the intersection of those social relationships that involve conflict over means and goals and in which at least one of the parties seeks to resolve the problem through resort to power. This identifies with control of livelihood and (economic) well-being, means of interpretation and means of coercion, the three classic sources of economic, ideological and coercive power.[54]

Politics as allocation

A further way of conceptualising politics is to focus on what it produces: on its outputs and results, on its effects. Many definitions of what politics is about refer to goals that we can immediately evaluate: public order, legality, good government and the distribution of collectively accumulated resources. Sometimes politics identifies with distinct outputs of these activities, such as specific 'policies'. More generally, it associates with the function of 'distributing values' within a given political community.

The best label for this vision springs from the title of a book that does not share it: *Politics: Who Gets What, When, How*.[55] Lasswell's influential book followed a different characterisation of politics (see the previous section),

---

53. Eckstein, H. (1973), 'Authority Patterns: A Structural Basis for Political Inquiry', *American Political Science Review*, 63: 1142–61. This was later elaborated in Eckstein, H. and T.R. Gurr (1975), *Patterns of Authority: A Structural Basis for Political Inquiry*, New York: Wiley.

54. Warren, M.E. (1999), 'What Is Political?', *Journal of Theoretical Politics*, 11: 207–31, esp. p. 217. Note, however, that this excellent article explicitly characterises politics in relation to the normative goals of democratic theory. This ends up setting arbitrary boundaries to the 'political', on the one hand, and adding unnecessary attributes to it, on the other hand. For instance, dominance, slavery, totalitarianism, hegemony and so forth are non-political to the extent that power is so overwhelming as to extinguish conflict. 'Where conflict does not exist we do not have politics, conflict is necessary for politics in combination with power', pp. 220–21.

55. Lasswell, H. (1936), *Politics: Who Gets What, When, How*, New York: McGraw Hill.

but its imaginative title best epitomises the school that defines politics via the actual values that are achieved through it (and by the identity of those who achieve them). What brings these conceptions together is a functional understanding of politics defined by means of its effects, and in particular its allocation effects.

David Easton is perhaps the most influential thinker in this line, although the many others who identify politics in functional terms may not share his systemic approach. Easton defines politics as the authoritative allocation by the political system of values for society: 'My point is, in summary, that the property of a social act *that informs it with a political aspect* is the act's relation to the authoritative allocation of values for a society' [my emphasis]. In turn, the political system consists of 'those interactions through which values are authoritatively allocated for a society'.[56]

By the word 'value', Easton means any sought-after goal in life, tangible or intangible. According to him, the basic functions of any political society are to allocate society's values and to obtain widespread acceptance of the authoritative, or binding, nature of the allocations. 'It is through the presence of activities that fulfil these two basic functions that a society can commit the resources and energies of its members in the settlement of differences that cannot be autonomously (i.e., individually or privately) resolved'.[57] To put it differently, Easton defines 'politics' as relating to the authoritative decisions of a society's government and to the effect that enforcement of these decisions has on the allocation, or distribution, of rewards and values among the different segments of the society.

The assimilation of politics to an allocative activity, to a production function, taps an undeniably essential dimension. There is no question that politics distributes 'values'. There can be doubt, however, about the legitimacy of characterising politics by its end results. In fact, the assimilation of 'politics' to a general acquisition or distribution activity leaves something to be desired. The wide-ranging extension of 'values' dangerously exposes politics to an overstretching of its content. In the Eastonian perspective, any fact, event or behaviour that happens to cross the boundaries of the political system, or to 'enter' the system and its production of 'values', is political. The consequence is that *whatever can contingently become politically 'relevant' is political*. The 'politicalness' of these facts, events and behaviours cannot in fact be defined but is entirely dependent on their capacity to cross the

---

56. Easton, David (1953), *The Political System: An Inquiry into the State of Political Science*, New York: Alfred A. Knopf, p. 134; Easton, David (1965), *A Systems Analysis of Political Life*, New York: John Wiley & Sons, p. 21.

57. Easton, David (1965), *A Framework for Political Analysis*, Englewood Cliffs, NJ: Prentice-Hall, p. 96.

boundaries of the political system. However, if behaviours are 'political' or 'non-political' because of their consequences, this leads to the conclusion that almost all behaviours can be regarded as politically relevant at some stage and in certain circumstances.[58]

Moreover, one cannot forget Schumpeter's lesson concerning economic activity. Few would deny that economic activity produces food, clothes and so on and that human beings need to eat to survive, and need clothes to protect themselves from the cold and so on. However, Schumpeter underlined the lack of realism of this perspective and sees the satisfaction of concrete needs as an unintended consequence of other drives, namely profit. In other words, the result of an activity does not necessarily constitute the motivational principle for the actor or therefore the explanation for his or her action.[59]

Politics as aggregation

The various aggregation approaches include all those visions of politics that with some simplification we can regroup under the rubric of 'economic theories of politics'. Under the assumptions that the actors worth considering are individuals, that they have preferences, that these preferences are mutually incompatible or jointly inconsistent and that not everybody can be simultaneously completely satisfied, the individuals engage in exchanges, threats, promises, agreements, coalitions and so on. The core problem of politics is identified in the procedures with which we allocate the scarce resources in a satisfactory way without reducing or eliminating the variety of interests and values.

Politics is functionally defined as the problem of aggregating prior and exogenous individual preferences into a collective choice. This tradition labels the interactions among actors and their (equilibrium) outcomes as 'political'. Due to the origins of this version of the definition in economics, 'politics' tends to be seen as a system of action in which individual preferences are aggregated through *voluntary* exchanges. The institutional and political arrangements resulting from these interactions are therefore conceptualised and evaluated primarily, if not exclusively, in terms of their capacity to achieve Pareto-optimal solutions. Discussion focuses on 'efficiency' in arranging these voluntary exchanges of resources. Problems of efficiency are in part due to (a) structural problems (i.e., externalities) and (b) subjective

---

58. See Finer, S.E. (1969–1970), 'Almond's Concept of "The Political System": A Textual Critique'.

59. Schumpeter, J.A. (1942, 3rd ed., 1949), *Capitalism, Socialism and Democracy*, London: Harper and Row, p. 282.

behavioural problems, such as problems of information, more or less complete rationality, agency and so on.

This view of politics can be summarised as follows: the political system is a decentralised exchange system that, subject to a number of constitutional constraints and a given distribution of endowments (positions, resources), eventually defines acceptable solutions. They are 'acceptable' because none or few of the actors can improve their standing from a personal point of view by acting unilaterally or with allies.

This line of thought tends to see the sphere of action of the political in constant comparison with other spheres of action that are not political – such as the market and the third sector of non-profit–driven social institutions – and for which the same evaluation criteria apply. Given that different individuals have different interests, positions and resources in these different spheres of action (politics, markets, non-profit third sector), and that the different spheres do not produce the same outcomes, individuals therefore have preferences as to the sphere which should be selected in which to decide the policies to be pursued. This view has quite a strong normative flavour, centred on the evaluation of the efficiency of the political sphere as compared to other 'non-political' spheres. This often leads to evaluating 'politics' as a mechanism for aggregating preferences which is alternative to markets and voluntary social institutions and to comparing it to the latter in terms of 'efficiency'.[60]

The version of the aggregation paradigm focusing on 'social dilemmas' deserves, perhaps, a separate mention. What is particular to the social dilemma version of the aggregation paradigm is the emphasis that it puts on the pervasive conflict between individual and group rationality. A set of participants in a social relationship have an option to contribute or not to a joint benefit. If everybody contributes, they achieve a net positive benefit. However, everybody has a temptation to shift from being a contributor to a non-contributor. The theoretical prediction is that everybody will do this and therefore not contribute. If this is the case, then the outcome will be a less valuable payoff, which, however, is a (Nash) equilibrium from which no one has an interest to move. The situation is a dilemma because an alternative exists that would yield a greater outcome for all the participants, but rational participants making isolated choices are not expected to realise this outcome.

Social dilemma studies are quite central to the contemporary discipline of political science. Unsurprisingly, social dilemmas frequently emerge when

---

60. This approach regards the distribution of endowments (rights, resources, competences, powers) as unproblematic; they are usually seen as properly allocated. Similarly, preferences lie outside the realm of the technical treatment of the function of aggregation. The same applies to problems of integrity. See March, James G. and Johan P. Olsen (1989), *Rediscovering Institutions. The Organisational Basis of Politics*, New York: The Free Press, p. 122.

humans are imagined as being without morals or ethical principles, unencumbered by social norms and conventions, uninterested in social honour or prestige, unaffected by love and hatred, insensitive to the lust for command and not prone to error. As Aristotle bluntly put it a long time ago, creatures of this kind must be either beasts or gods,[61] and for such entities almost any social relationship turns into a social dilemma, and social dilemmas pop up anytime and anywhere.[62] However, this is of no concern here, where the focus is on the conception of the political that derives from these premises.

In this perspective, the problem that remains in the shadow is the origin of 'sanctions'. In social dilemmas, the option of introducing sanctions to punish non-cooperators or to keep agreements is not available. The action of sanctioning constitutes new public goods and generates a second-order dilemma of equal or even greater difficulty, in an endless regression. Under these conditions, the possibility of avoiding the negative outcome of social dilemmas is linked to the possibility of the players achieving self-enforcing equilibria by committing themselves to punish non-cooperators sufficiently severely to deter non-cooperation. That is, sanctions must be generated by the game and within the game. Alternatively, one can work towards constituting different models of choice theory that include trust, reciprocity, reputations, norms, roles and so forth and that apply without an external authority offering inducements or imposing sanctions. In specific conditions, people can establish rules and sanctions by themselves. In particular, when dealing with pooled common resources, individuals may be willing to act collectively to change the institutional structure of the game.[63] In any case, it seems that these schemes may at best generate sanctions only within the interacting set of actors. A broader sanctioning system can result only from a mysterious deus ex machina exogenous to the model: the state. The 'state' is seen as an authority that is constituted in functional terms: to solve social dilemmas for everybody whenever they fail to solve them otherwise. But it remains puzzling where such a benevolent institution comes from within the anthropological assumptions of this paradigm. The solution reintroduces through the windows what it discharged from the door. If the state has always existed, it

---

61. 'But he who is unable to live in society, and who has no need because he is sufficient for himself, must be either a beast or a god'. Aristotle (350 BC; 2013), *Politics*, Book 1, Chapter 2, p. 55.

62. This leads to the criticism that 'orientations' unlike selfishness have developed exactly because no one can live in a constant social dilemma, an argument developed in Green, Donald P. and Ian Schapiro (1994), *Pathologies of Rational Choice Theories. A Critique of Applications in Political Science*, New Haven, CT: Yale University Press.

63. Olstrom has consistently worked in this direction. See Olstrom, Elinor (1990), *Governing the Commons*, Cambridge: Cambridge University Press; and Olstrom, Elinor (2010), 'Beyond Markets and States: Polycentric Governance and Complex Economic Systems', *American Economic Review*, 100: 1–33.

could defeat social dilemma situations by its sheer presence; if it is not there, it is hard to imagine how it could help to solve lower-order social dilemmas.

From the point of view that interests us here, models of social dilemmas may be made more realistic, but they remain limited to the interactions and to the sanctions spontaneously generated by a set of independent actors. In this view, politics is the sphere of interactions deprived of authority structures. Politics identified with social dilemmas redefines the political by expelling its most distinctive features: authority and command. When conceived as a spontaneous generation of order and authority among a set of independent autonomous actors, the political appears to have a benign nature.

WHY A CONTINUING DEBATE?

The previous succinct discussion of contemporary conceptions of the political has identified six large families which respectively emphasise 'activities', 'locations', 'conflict', 'means' (power/coercion), 'allocative outcomes' and the 'aggregation of preferences'. Why do we need further reflection with such a variety available to us? I have three claims of relevance, two of which are strictly scientific, while the third relates to the connection between the study of politics and current developments in the world.

My first claim is that most if not all the conceptions of 'politics' discussed previously offer a general definition of politics encompassing all its phenomenology. In so doing, they often fall into functional definitions: what politics does, produces, distributes and so on. Such definitions do not rest on an underlying theory of individual political action as a starting point and from which to reconstruct more complex macro-outcomes. I would like to explore this latter neglected perspective. It is interesting to note that almost all the scholars I have mentioned deny the possibility of constructing a theory of politics starting from a motivational basis.[64] I propose to discuss this issue anew and to investigate whether a motivational theory of political action is possible and whether it can logically connect to other key political questions. In other words, I do not start from what 'politics' as a field, sphere or activity is or does but rather from an

---

64. Sartori does this explicitly. Warren rejects the conception of politics as a kind of 'behaviour', assuming that this rules out any primary reference to intentional states, actions or social relationships. He therefore seems to equate the term 'behaviour' with a specific methodological school. However, his definition does not refer to 'political action' either. Warren, M.E. (1999), 'What Is Political?', *Journal of Theoretical Politics*, 11: 207–31, p. 210. Most other scholars are less explicit in their attitude to political behaviour (or political action) as a foundation for a theory of politics. To the best of my knowledge, only de Jouvenel and Stoppino follow him and explicitly pursue this line of reasoning, in part at least.

interpretation of what individual 'nuclear' or 'elementary' political action is from a motivational point of view. Once this elementary individual political action is defined with reference to other types of action (in chapter 2), I will proceed to specify its variety of forms depending on the fields in which it manifests itself (chapters 3 and 4). Finally, in chapter 5 I will come back to the question of what politics is and try to reconstruct its overall complex phenomenology from the viewpoint of the definition of individual political action.

My second claim is that the six predominant approaches often try to define different things at the same time. We search for the unique predicaments that characterise any a priori non-given group in its constitution as a political entity. Within a so-defined group, we are concerned to identify the confining conditions that define the political in the area that extends between the sheer violence of the state of nature and the private synallagmatic[65] dealings of unconnected and non-confined individuals free to determine their outcomes through unilateral action. We engage in the identification of the specific and essential element of individual political action and its difference from other motivations. We discuss the specific means and essential instruments with which politics operates. We also define politics functionally, via its 'production': what it achieves and what it is useful for. There is a resemblance between these questions and the traditions I have briefly outlined in this chapter, but it is unlikely that any single family accurately addresses all the questions.

I propose to proceed by separating these issues but linking them in an analytical and logically consistent way, so that the answer to any question may logically derive from that provided for the previous one. This requires political theory to be built on the foundation of a single solid rock to which all other reasoning can be traced. I propose that this solid rock be a definition of nuclear or elementary political behaviour (or action) in its motivational dimension. In the following chapters, I will carry out this 'unpacking' of the political phenomenon. Proceeding in this way, I will return to some of the approaches to politics discussed briefly in the introduction and discuss them more thoroughly. However, rather than seeing these approaches as alternative attempts at a general definition of the political, I will order them along a ladder of abstraction that may account for the variety of specifically political experiences.

---

65. I introduce here, and will use throughout the rest of this book, the outmoded terms 'synallagma' and 'synallagmatic' to refer to pure deals among autonomous and unconfined parties bounded only by reciprocal obligations. Later (pp. 120–21), it will be shown that the term 'contract' is misleading, as it implicitly includes far more than a mutual obligation among parties.

I will try to define 'politics'

- by identifying the minimal characteristic element of nuclear political behaviour with respect to other behaviours via an analysis of motivations;
- in terms of the nature of the environmental conditions that transform and differentiate such nuclear political behaviour;
- in terms of the unique predicaments that political behaviours generate in the constitution of aggregate political entities;
- in terms of the specific means with which politics operates; and
- in terms of the single-value that politics generates.

It is necessary to link 'motivations', 'conditions', 'predicaments', 'means' and 'outcomes' in a framework of progressive specification which underlies the connections among them. Rather than characterising politics in terms of praxeological manifestations, loci, means or functions, I would like to achieve the opposite result: to derive the specific activities, 'locations' and contingent manifestations from the analytical characteristics are identified. This may lead to a few rather counterintuitive and controversial results emerging.

Finally, let me advance a few more mundane reasons why it is not advisable to abandon the question of the nature of politics in the garret of our cognitively mobilised, organisationally dense and pluralistic 'societies'. In the current state of the discipline of political science, continuing the debate may have positive methodological or perhaps therapeutic effects on the knowledge enterprise undertaken by political scientists. The debate clearly spells out the underlying assumptions of different conceptions of politics which are definitely 'historical'. A characterisation of what is political is part of political science, not only as a mere ex ante definition of its subject but also as a continuing reflection on the substance of politics in each historical period. This is particularly important in view of the complex relations, which were alluded to at the beginning of this chapter, between the political and the many disciplines that legitimately include them within their scope: philosophy, sociology, law, history, economics and anthropology. The mushrooming of highly specialised and technically hyper-sophisticated studies has led to a poor level of exchange and communication within the discipline. If direct exchange is difficult, a meta-debate about what is politically relevant and about the 'political' relevance of the stories we are telling can represent an element of unity for the discipline.

Moreover, in the last three or four decades 'politics' has come under attack. In the post-WWII period, an alliance among anti-capitalist social groups, bureaucratic elites and elected political officials successfully shaped the regulatory cage to make capital nationally 'responsible' and dependent'.[66] In the last quarter of the twentieth century, this statist trend came under attack from holders of economic resources who felt damaged by the negotiated agreements they had been forced to accept. Neoliberal ideas overtook the economic expectations that emerged among the Western publics after the long phase of *étatism* and Keynesianism. A worldwide network of private institutions (including high-grade research institutes and universities) and personnel in leading positions in both national and international economic institutions communicated these ideas and deeply influenced the media. Large sections of national electorates evidenced increasing concern over growing fiscal burdens and misgivings about management or mismanagement of public funds by the political personnel. This justified and supported a reversal of the relationship between political power and economic power. State intervention should stop charging society for its costs. The political elite was advised to adopt a measure of self-denial.[67] A subordination of the political to the economic (and to the social) had never been so explicitly advocated. Politics was redefined as a supporting activity and ancillary knowledge for the maintenance of the efficiency of markets, and policies are now predominantly the result of collusion between the political class as a whole and the commanding economic forces.[68] My preoccupation lies in the observation that this outcome may not be stable. Tensions are unlikely to reverberate on the markets themselves; they will instead reverberate through politics, which is likely to be asked to provide the stabilising mechanisms for unstable economies and societies. Signs are accumulating of a turning point, with renewed requests for the political to rescue the unchained Prometheus of the market from excessive expectations about its capacity of self-regulation. In such a situation of discredited politics and states, the means and instruments that can be deployed to this end are a source of serious concern.

Finally, the question of the nature of politics is still relevant, necessary and pertinent today because in the geographical area of the West the seventy years since WWII have made a vision of politics as a successfully 'domesticated' domain predominant. This state of affairs may be neither permanent nor generalisable to the rest of the world. A (temporary?) attenuation of the interstate rivalries that have ravaged the modern era has reduced people's feelings of physical insecurity. Impressive economic growth and the feeling that we can manage production, distribution and consumption crises have reduced the

---

66. Bartolini, S. (2005), *Restructuring Europe. Centre Formation, System Building and Political Structuring between the Nation State and the EU*, Oxford: Oxford University Press, p. 109.

67. On this point, see the arguments in Strange, S. (1995), 'The Limits of Politics', *Government and Opposition*, 30: 291–311.

68. Mair, P. (2013), *Ruling the Void. The Hollowing of Western Democracy*, New York: Verso.

dilemmas of hunger and deprivation. Advances in science and technology and a disenchantment and secularisation of our societies have somehow displaced the existential dilemma of personal insignificance and cosmic meaningless. The attenuation of these inescapable human vulnerabilities[69] in the West has made political science somehow less sensitive to and less interested in the dark side of politics, in the evil face of domination and violence and in the role of powerful ideologies.[70] The idea that the rest of the world is simply *en marche* towards the same values has further contributed to focalising political science on specialised analyses of interstitial political phenomena, narrow policies and a restricted range of behaviour, with overemphasis on individual autonomy and an optimistic faith in reasoning and dialogic learning as a basis for collective outcomes. Nevertheless, in large parts of the world, politics is still unchained and undomesticated, and so we should wonder how representative our concerns for these realities are. We should perhaps leave room for less benign variants. This is not an act of condescension. It is a reminder that things change, that nothing in human affairs is guaranteed and secured forever and that vulnerabilities re-emerge; that is, in politics, the dark side is always burning under the ashes of favourable circumstances.

---

69. These are the vulnerabilities to which Popitz links the phenomenology of different forms of power. Popitz, H. (1992, 2nd ed.), *Phaenomene der Macht*, Tubingen: J.C.B. Mohr.

70. What Ritter labelled the *demoniac face of politics*. Ritter, Gerhard (1948; 1940), *Die Dämonie der Macht*, München: Verlag G.R. Oldenbourg.

Chapter 2

Nuclear political action

The terms 'political behaviour' and 'political action' are recent and do not appear in the history of political thought. The former is usually associated with the behaviourist approach in political science developed in the 1920s, mainly at the University of Chicago under the leadership of Charles E. Merriman, Harold Lasswell, Herbert Simon and others. However, the term did not appear in the title of a book until the Swedish political scientist Herbert Tingsten used it for his ground-breaking study of electoral statistics in 1937.[1] Since then, 'political behaviour' has become the standard title for courses in micro-political analysis. The way I use the term 'behaviour' here does not refer to this methodological approach and the behaviourist 'revolution' so magnificently outlined by Robert A. Dahl at his zenith.[2] Nor do I intend to oppose 'behaviour' to 'action', implying a stronger sense of intentionality carried by the latter as opposed to the former. In this context, I use them as synonyms.

I address the question of whether a distinct motivation for behaviour (action) exists that can be called 'political' and distinguished from other modalities. In a prosaic sense, we usually consider 'legislative behaviour', 'voting behaviour' and 'protest behaviour' to be 'political behaviours'; that is, we most often label as political behaviour specific activities. Nevertheless, this is a pedestrian labelling which tells us nothing about what is 'political' about voting, legislating and protesting. The adjective 'political' can be added to an infinite number of other terms, but the nature of the 'politicalness' needs to be defined independently of the object or activity to which it applies.

---

1. Tingsten, Herbert (1937), *Political Behaviour: Studies in Election Statistics*, London: P. S. King.
2. Dahl, R. (1961), 'The Behavioral Approach in Political Science: Epitaph for a Monument to a Successful Protest', *American Political Science Review* 55: 763–73.

My question is whether and under which circumstances the motivation for action can define the political element in behaviour *from the individual point of view*. To put it briefly, I intend to define which category of action is specifically political.

Reference to 'motivation' generates a set of very complex issues. Motivation may refer to deep actor 'orientation' such as egotism, altruism and aggressiveness. Others argue that motivation simply reflects the normative and cultural environment that shapes actors' identities. There are competing psychological theories of motivation as inner needs that have to be successively satisfied.[3] Controversy surrounds the question of whether motivations should be seen as conscious orientations or as unreflexive drives.[4] Different perspectives stress that we know nothing about motivations, and we need to focus on preferences as expressed or revealed through choices. It should be understood that I will not discuss any of these complex theoretical issues in this context. I do not have the intellectual instruments to face them. Moreover, for my purpose it may not be necessary. For my limited perspective, it is enough to accept that 'motivation' is a theoretical construct of the observer to interpret the behaviour of the observed. Here, I will limit myself to a parsimonious list of motivations that social scientists usually 'attribute' to individuals in the attempt to understand their behaviour. I will briefly discuss these motivational categories before coming to the question that interests me: whether we can construct a motivational category for interpreting the behaviours that we call 'political'. It is important to stress that different motivations also differentiate actions and qualify certain disciplinary approaches.

THE CATEGORIES OF ACTION: INTEREST, MORALITY AND HONOUR

The interest category

Interest has always been seen as a powerful motivator of human action. In his marvellous fresco of sixteenth-century Spanish society, Miguel de Cervantes makes 'interest' introduce himself straightforwardly with these powerful words: *Soy quien puede mas que amor*.[5] Through interest, human action is understood in relation to material rewards or costs. A body of legal norms sets

---

3. Such as the Maslowian differentiation between biological, security, attachment, esteem, cognitive, aesthetic, self-actualisation and transcendence needs; Maslow, A.H. (1943), 'A Theory of Human Motivation', *Psychological Review*, 50: 370–96.

4. This issue is at the core of the successful book by Haidt, Jonathan (2012), *The Righteous Mind. Why Good People Are Divided by Politics and Religion*, New York: Pantheon Books.

5. 'I am more powerful than love' (author's translation): de Cervantes, Miguel (1911–1913; 1605), *El ingenioso hidalgo don Quijote de la Mancha*, Madrid: Ediciones de la lectura, p. 569.

out permitted and forbidden actions and provides penalties for various types of the forbidden ones. In a situation of alternatives for scarce goods, actions can be seen as motivated by the maximisation of gains (or the limitation of losses) and interpreted as resulting from calculations driven by the criteria of 'utility'. In any case, human actions are constrained within a repertory by considering costs and gains. Any further elaboration of the concept of interest would lead us far away from my concern here. I limit my scanty notes to the non-contextual and non-relational nature of this motivational category in its pure analytical form.[6]

Basically, 'interest' is the analytical category of economics and law, or, more precisely, of individuals' economic and legal behaviour. Economists have other ways to define their discipline than resorting to utility. The literature makes frequent reference to the science of scarcity, of maximising behaviour and of choice.[7] Nonetheless, it is fair to argue that, as far as the *individual* actor's economic behaviour is concerned, utility calculations and drives are dominant, and they remain the benchmarking assumptions even in those macroeconomic studies that rely less on micro-motivation specifications.

Lawyers also have good reasons to oppose the idea that the production, interpretation and adjudication of law can be reduced to considerations and calculations of utility. To the extent that law is primarily conceived as orders backed by sanctions,[8] as rules forbidding or encouraging certain types of behaviours with associated penalties, it can be seen as setting the terms for individuals' utility calculations regarding the penalties involved in its violation. Similarly, in the production and even the interpretation of law, rationalistic visions prevail concerning the way in which individuals react to norms according to their advantages and disadvantages. Unquestionably, the web of formal rules represents a behavioural map for individuals with associated costs and advantages of following the prescribed routes as opposed to searching for shortcuts.

However, there are varieties of formal rules that do not fit this description. In particular, this is the case of those norms and statutes that are different in

---

6. For an analytical review of the concept of 'interest', the best sources are Neuendorff, Hartmut (1973), *Der Begriff des Interesses. Eine Studie zu den Gesellschaftstheorien von Hobbes, Smith und Marx*, Frankfurt: Suhrkamp; Ornaghi, Lorenzo and Silvio Cotellessa (2000), *Interesse*, Bologna: Il Mulino; and Hirschman, A.O. (1977), *The Passions and the Interests. Political Arguments for Capitalism before Its Triumph*, Princeton, NJ: Princeton University Press. See also Bluditt, T.M. (1975), 'The Concept of Interest in Political Theory', *Political Theory*, 3: 245–58.

7. See Coase, Ronald H. (1978), 'Economics and Contiguous Disciplines', *Journal of Legal Studies*, 7: 201–11; Backhouse, Roger E. and Steven Medema (2009), 'Retrospectives: On the Definition of Economics', *Journal of Economic Perspectives*, 23: 221–33.

8. As in Austin's classic shortcut: Austin, John (1832), *The Province of Jurisprudence Determined*, London: John Murray.

character from the 'rule backed by threat of sanction', in the sense that they do not require people to do or not do things but confer powers and prerogatives on them. In this perspective, to see law as orders backed by sanctions ends up imposing on the variety of laws a spurious uniformity that conceals more than it reveals.[9] The question remains open whether, in the end, a law that confers rights and prerogatives also rests on the assumption that its violation *by other individuals* leads to sanctions. We will come back to norms 'conferring powers' at a later part of this book. Here, we can accept the plurality of legal instruments but insist that, *from the point of view of individual behaviour* – and thus leaving in the background the nature of law as such – the legal order is probably the most powerful cognitive map for calculating costs and advantages.[10]

Note that in its pure form the motivational category of interest is *non-relational*. It only depends on individual calculations that are independent of concrete relevant others and of the relations one entertains with them.[11] Pure-form interest motivations are also *non-contextual*. They are independent of the socio-cultural context in which they take place and are unaffected by it. In other words, the potential consequences for others and the cultural influence of the environment are exogenous to specific calculations of utility.

The moral category

In contrast to interest-driven action, the pure form of moral behaviour rests on no calculations. This human motivation leads to acting in pursuit of 'good'. The motivational criteria is 'morality'; that is, an adherence to a set of internalised norms that are effective determinants of action. Without entering into the contested field of definitions of universal human morality, we refer here to the list of widely shared cross-cultural moral principles discussed by anthropologists and moral psychologists.[12] What we call 'moral' is that

---

9. For the debate on the nature of law and for these specific points, see Hart, H. L. A. (1994, 2nd ed.; 1st ed. 1961), *The Concept of Law*, Oxford: Clarendon, p. 3 and p. 48.

10. 'The most prominent general feature of law at all times and places is that its existence means that certain kinds of human conduct are no longer optional, but in *some* sense obligatory'; Hart, H. L. A. (1994), *The Concept of Law*, p. 6.

11. It may be argued that this vision of the interest motivation best describes games against nature, while it does not apply to strategic games, where in pursuing an interest one is obliged to take into account expectations about relevant others' behaviour. However, consideration of relevant others pertains to the strategy of pursuing your interests, not to defining them, which does not depend on them. This is the sense in which I believe that the category of interest, as an analytical category, is non-relational.

12. Such as Brown, Donald (1991), *Human Universals*, New York: McGraw-Hill; and Haidt, J. (2001), 'The Emotional Dog and Its Rational Tail. A Social Intuitionist Approach to Moral Judgement', *Psychological Review*, 108: 814–34. For an overview of the overall debate in this field, see Young, Liane and Rebecca Saxe (2011), 'Moral Universals and Individual Differences', *Emotion Review*, 3: 323–24.

special form of respect for yourself that imposes certain behaviours irrespective of the presence of relevant others and of their possibility of knowing about such behaviours. Moral action is effectively independent of relevant others and it is unrelated to them; that is, it is non-relational. Morally driven behaviour would be the same whether it were performed in front of a relevant set of others or in total solitude. Moral behaviour is also little influenced by the social context (the universality mentioned before); that is, in its pure form it is non-contextual. From the latter two points of view it resembles utility-driven behaviour, as both are unaffected by the presence of others and the nature of such others.

These similarities have allowed rational choice approaches to intrude into the domain of moral behaviour, modelling moral rules deriving from prisoner's dilemmas with an exit option, with the option not to play, which yields a payoff inferior to cooperation but superior to defection.[13] However, the pure form of action driven by moral norms described here makes it independent of any specific interaction pattern or any learning and reciprocity in repeated games. The fact that moral behaviour is independent of others – relevant or irrelevant – by definitional fiat rules out the application of strategic dyadic games to its analysis. If the moral behaviour of an individual depends on an expectation and learning that the other will also behave morally, then there is no need to distinguish moral behaviour from any other form of strategic behaviour.

The honour category

In many cases, more numerous than is usually recognised, we become motivated to do something by the way in which we expect others to react to what we do. People do or do not do certain things because it would jeopardise or enhance their image in the eyes of others, something we often – very often indeed – care about. Here, I define defending the image of oneself *in the eyes of relevant others* as a third basic motivational category: 'honour'.

A profound and lasting preoccupation with respect is a characteristic of human beings.[14] Every individual usually cares about being *worthy of respect*.

---

13. For the game theoretical tradition, see Gauthier, David (1986), *Morals by Agreements*, Oxford: Clarendon Press.
14. Note that one can respect another person in two ways. *Appraisal respect* relates to skills and performance, and it implies positively judging a person according to certain standards (e.g., we respect Federer for his tennis talent). I am not interested here in this form of competitive performance respect, or 'esteem'. *Recognition respect*, on the other hand, does not imply having a high opinion of specific abilities or skills but instead approaching and treating people in such a way as to give the right weight to their role or position. Recognition respect is the object of 'honour' and reflects a positive consideration of the person that it recognises. See Appiah, Kwame Anthony (2010), *The Honour Code. How Moral Revolutions Happen*, New York: W. W. Norton and Co., p. XIII.

Neuroscience and evolutionary psychology theory consider that this inclination towards 'social morality' is innate in human beings and in the distant past was probably associated with considerable rewards.[15] People invest considerable resources in their search for this form of respect as 'honour'; they suffer losses, and they sometimes go as far as risking their lives. People motivated by the sense of honour can violate legal rules and moral norms and can do things that negatively affect their material interests. Nevertheless, we should not reserve the category of honour-based behaviour to extreme cases. We do or do not undertake a very large number of daily actions in view of the blame or praise they generate which affects our image in the eyes of the people we care about. From the point of view of the individual, defence of one's own social honour demands that one adheres to the standard that it sets. This is social 'reputation'. The sentiment that accompanies dishonourable social behaviour is 'shame'; and what others feel about somebody who has done something dishonourable is 'contempt'. Loss of honour is perceived as a loss of the right to respect. Therefore, honour is inherently and unquestionably relational. It engages us only when we are in public, under the eyes of other human beings, and in particular of those human beings whose respect we value, or when we expect relevant others to know of our actions, even if they are performed in solitude.

Honour is also contextual.[16] Defining who we ask for and expect respect from is crucial. Usually, this is not all humanity but a special social group. A code of social honour is different to a moral code because it is socially contingent and determined by the relevant social groups whose respect we seek. This means that honour can sustain and motivate opposite actions depending on the context of the relevant others. It is socially changing and is not embodied in any given set of values or norms, not even within a general culture. The same behaviour can be regarded as worthy of respect or unworthy of respect, honourable or dishonourable, according to the context and the code of the reference social group.[17]

Some sociologists may resist the idea that 'honour' is the typical category of understanding in sociology, but few would disagree that it is a central motivational concern for the discipline. Often, it is identified by the concept of 'status'. However, here I prefer the term 'honour' as my perspective focuses on the motivations of individual actors rather than on the general honour stratification principles of any community. One could argue that all

---

15. See Gazzaniga, Michael (2011), *Who Is in Charge? Free Will and the Science of the Brain*, New York: HarperCollins Publishers.

16. Anderson Stewart, Frank (1994), *Honor*, Chicago: University of Chicago Press, pp. 44–47.

17. For example, in the context of a mafia-dominated situation, defence of your self-image in the eyes of relevant others may push you to do things that in a different context are regarded as highly dishonourable. Honourable behaviour is not moral, just or adequate behaviour.

those identities based on religion, ethnicity, nationality, class and gender are usually associated with a sense of honour. If collective identities shape the sense of individual honour, then this opens the door to the possibility that we can share the honour or the dishonour of the persons with whom we identify.

Honour, therefore, does not correspond to morality. However, a certain kind of honour is the right to respect acquired by following the principles of morality: a code of honour that attributes respect to the fact that you do your own moral duty. In this case, honour and duty are likely to coincide. Another type of honour is the right to respect that derives from acting beyond what morality demands. This kind of supererogatory behaviour pushes people to act in a way that is morally desirable but demands too much to be morally mandatory (e.g., a heroic sacrifice of yourself or of your dearest relatives, friends).

Interest, honour and morality

I conclude this section with a few considerations concerning the three pure types. The interest, moral and the honour criteria as described earlier are *pure* types of motivation to interpret action or non-action, although it is easy to contaminate one with the others. The three categories constitute the interpretative tools of the social sciences. Law and economics focus primarily on the system of incentives which are external (exogenous) to the actors that shape their actions. Moral philosophy, psychology and sociology predominantly focus on the system of internal incentives that may shape the same actions.

Note that in principle these three categories can explain the same action. Facing the actual possibility of stealing a pen in a shop, an external observer could interpret the fact that the person eventually did not steal by resorting to any of the criteria. We can interpret that the interest in and the reward from the non–paid-for pen were not worth the risks and possible consequences (the person calculates the consequence of the action if discovered). We can also imagine that the marginal utility was too low (if she decided to face the risks involved in stealing, then she would rather steal something else). You could argue, however, that notwithstanding a strong interest in the pen and the fact that legal penalties would be unlikely in this specific circumstance, the person did not steal the pen because she was concerned about what her close friends would think of her if they knew she was a thief. If the non-stealing occurs notwithstanding a strong interest in the object, an unlikeliness of associated penalties and the absence of relevant others in front of whom social honour could be at stake, we can conclude that deep internalised norms impede the action. In this way, a moral motivation superimposes itself above any other type of evaluation of the situation. In many cases, a close analysis of the contest helps to disentangle the motivation drive, but causal statements about action or non-action are often very difficult. Some disciplines solve the problem by making an assumption about which drive is dominant.

Honour and morality have a crucial function in every human aggregate. In many if not most cases, incentive systems based on material rewards and legal punishments are insufficient to achieve social outcomes that we deem desirable. In most cases, whatever expensive efforts we can make to provide an incentive for desirable behaviour or to guarantee a form of surveillance over the undesirable ones, the expected behaviour is not guaranteed unless a form of social honour and/or a sense of moral duty intervene. Rationally devised incentives and punishments may be ineffective against deeply felt honour codes. Honour and morality are forces that operate over a long distance without the need for specific mechanisms of ex ante incentives or ex post surveillance, that is, even in the absence of a system of law or a system of economic compensation. The specific case of many professional roles is a suitable example. It is very hard to evaluate and control how conscientiously doctors, teachers, financial advisors, judges and others behave. We hope that they do not limit themselves to behavioural models that simply avoid legal punishment or a risk of economic losses. If honour and morality are present, they enormously reduce the costs of incentives and surveillance. However, the cost of generating honour/morality is hard to know and a comparison with the cost of legal and economic incentives is hard to make. This is why in contemporary societies there is an embedded tendency to invest more in legal and economic inducements than in the production and maintenance of morality and honour.

In fact, the category of personal interest has recently expanded to interpret a growing number of behaviours. The general and neutral concept of 'utility' – where utility stands for whatever you may aspire to or desire or need, and as such contains all pleasures or pains – extends to cover all other possible motivations.[18] Fear of sanctions is an element in your utility calculations as a negative incentive. Internalised norms concerning 'good' can be conceptualised as nothing other than preferences. Similarly, the social esteem that you aim at preserving or increasing in your environment is nothing other than something you like and praise and therefore part of your preference structure and utility considerations.[19] This imperial drive of the utility category has

---

18. For an explicit choice in this direction and a discussion of its justification, see Mantzavinos, C. (2001), *Individuals, Institutions, and Markets*, Cambridge: Cambridge University Press, pp. 10–15.

19. Some authors formulate this position in a slightly different way by distinguishing 'self-interest' from 'interest' and making the first a subcategory of the second: 'Interest, understood as a general category only points (independently of the nature of the motivations: egoistic, altruistic or of a different type) to a disposition to act in view of the achievement of a purpose that the actor deems worth achieving'. Panebianco, Angelo (2009), *L'automa e lo spirito. Azioni individuali, istituzioni, imprese collettive*, Bologna: Il Mulino, p. 85 (my translation). If every action with a goal or purpose is defined as interest-driven, then only purposeless and therefore foolish or insane actions are not.

been going on for quite a while in the social sciences, and it will take some time to see whether it will lead to triviality or to an integrated utility-based social science of some significance.

The solution of transforming every motivation into a single utility (or interest) dimension generates, however, a host of empirical problems. Consider the following paradigmatic example: In a post office queue, the first in the line is an elderly pensioner with plenty of time and visibly not much money, while the last is a young yuppie with considerable income and little time. Following a utility approach, an agreement can be realised in which the pensioner and the yuppie negotiate an exchange of places for an adequate remuneration, while the utilities of all the intermediate people in the queue remain unchanged. Although Pareto-optimal, this exchange of places based on marginal utility theory rarely (if ever) occurs in practice. If attempted, it is likely to encounter scandalised reactions from the intermediate people, although their utility is unaltered by the exchange between the first and the last in the queue (and, for that matter by any other similar exchange that does not affect the relative position of the others). In other words, it involves an honour issue for the applicant, the respondent and all the other people involved in the social relation. If such an exchange is realised, it usually takes the form of a polite request to all the other people in the queue justified by some special reasons and as a matter of courtesy. If we assume that the search for honour is also a utility search, and if we do not distinguish honour motivation from utility motivations, how could we explain the outcome? If the exchange takes place (on the basis of pure interest) or does not happen (based on pure honour), in both cases the actors would maximise their 'utility'. Here, utility drives both the Pareto-optimal and the Pareto-suboptimal solutions. Should we engage in differentiating among different kinds of utility? If we do so, the advantage is lost, as different utilities are not much better than different motivations.

THE POLITICAL CATEGORY

Is there a motivational category that underlies political actions? The challenge is to identify the nuclear or elementary action that deserves to be defined as 'political' through its motivational underpinning.

A first reaction is that political action does not rest on any special and different motivation. Political action is subject to the same exogenous and endogenous determinants such as the search for material rewards, the adherence to moral norms and the search for social honour. In this sense, we cannot speak of *political behaviour* except in a metaphorical sense: 'When we examine the facts more closely, what strikes us most is the great variety of motives that steer political behaviour. . . . "Political behaviour" should not be understood literally. The expression does not point to any particular type of behaviour'.[20]

I am not satisfied with this dominant view. I suggest that there is a sense in which we can identify the specific motivation for 'political' action. Unlike all other motivational drives, political action is that type of action whose aim is to achieve the obedience, the acquiescence or the acceptance of other actors. More precisely, the desire to get somebody else to do something that he or she would not otherwise have done, or to not do something that he or she would otherwise have done, motivates political action. 'Deciding over the others' is the key and the distinctive element. Political action is action motivated by a search for the behavioural compliance of relevant others. By following this route, I approach, at least in part, those conceptions of politics that identify it with power in the tradition of Lasswell, hints of politics as action by man over man from Bertrand de Jouvenel, the pages by Mario Stoppino devoted to political action[21] and the concept of 'directiveness' as elaborated by Frohock.[22] In particular, I am indebted to Frohock's way of framing the problem. In his view, there are core terms or fixed structures of invariant properties that are common to all instances of the political, which is exactly what I am trying to define here.[23] Frohock identifies these core terms for politics as 'directiveness' – agents acting on one another and directing one another's behaviour – and 'aggregations' – collections of agents as the units acting in politics. Aggregation is not part of my argument here,[24] but I see a considerable similarity between my conception of the political as the search for behavioural compliance and Frohock's core term 'directiveness', and I agree with his point that, when this core term is not there, there is a change of meaning of politics. Politics ceases to exist if this core term is withdrawn from it.[25] Let me pursue my elaboration of the line of thought of these authors and push it a bit further.

---

20. Sartori, G. (1973), 'What Is "Politics"', *Political Theory*, 1: 17.
21. Lasswell, H.D. and A. Kaplan (1950), *Power and Society*, New Haven, CT: Yale University Press; de Jouvenel, Bertrand (1963), *The Pure Theory of Politics*, Cambridge: Cambridge University Press; Stoppino, M. (2001; 1995), *Potere e teoria politica*, Milano: Giuffré.
22. Frohock, F.M. (1978), 'The Structure of Politics', *American Political Science Review*, 72: 859–70.
23. Ibid., pp. 866–77. However, he refuses to define this as the essence of the political in Schmitt's sense.
24. 'Aggregation' defines the type of interaction among actors, and it suggests that politics requires actors to engage in forced interaction and therefore to 'aggregate'. As will become clear in my following treatment, the conditions for free or forced interaction are crucial to my further definition of the environmental conditions that differentiate requests for behavioural compliance. However, it is not necessary to deal with this point at this stage.
25. Frohock makes a telling example: 'Or imagine a world (like the one Adam Smith imagined) where no direction of human behaviour takes place. Things just happen in a happy state of nature of natural coordination (or independent movement) with no one ever "getting" anyone to do anything. ... Such a world has no referential use for the language of "politics". Such terms as "authority",

In everyday language, acquiescence, compliance, conformity and obedience are often synonymous. Only psychologists have amply debated the various mechanisms at the roots of compliance and conformity.[26] They tend to define compliance as a particular kind of response – acquiescence – to a particular kind of communication taking the form of a 'request', either explicit or implicit. Acquiescence is therefore the act or condition of giving tacit assent – agreement or consent by silence or without objection. Conformity, on the other hand, points to a change in behaviour to match the responses of others and to the desire to achieve a correct interpretation of reality and behave correctly and to obtain social approval from others. In this case, social psychologists seem to follow the common language use in that conformity is an act by conformists of adaptation to prevailing norms and standards. Social psychology does not use the term 'obedience' when explicitly referring to the direct exercise of authority, command and hierarchy. It prefers to use the term 'social influence', thus focusing on more subtle mechanisms.

However, even obedience has several meanings. These include obedience as an automatic, un-reflected-upon, almost spontaneous habit of submitting to somebody else's will; obedience as a calculation of the costs and advantages of obedience versus non-obedience in terms of the probability and significance of possible sanctions; and obedience grounded in a sense of moral obligation. Hence, we could have three concepts: *acquiescence* (which is tacit), *conformity* (as adherence and compliance) and *obedience* (pointing to a more direct response to commands). Being unwilling to make a definite choice among these meanings, I am interested in arriving at a general term that represents all the forms that range from acceptance to acquiescence to conformity to obedience. In the remainder of this book I will employ the term *behavioural compliance* to indicate and include these various forms.

First, elementary political action defined as the search for compliance *needs to be intentional*, that is, aimed at achieving the compliance sought after. Unintended consequences for others do not qualify an action as political, although they may be momentous in political analysis. If A modifies B's behaviour without explicitly aiming to do so, the result does not qualify A's action as 'political'. Second, *the types of goals and final value aimed at do not define political action*. Whether actor A aims at wealth, support, help, a favourable decision or whatever else, her action can be defined as political to

---

the "state", "sovereignty" and so on do not describe anything intelligible in non-directive words. . . . A change from directive to non-directive social units, or from aggregate to singular units, significantly affects all other terms in political language, shifts the meaning of politics altogether and perhaps even makes the concept meaningless'. Frohock, 'The Structure of Politics', p. 866.

26. For recent psychological research developments in this field, see Cialdini, Robert B. and Noah J. Goldstein (2004), 'Social Influence: Compliance and Conformity', *Annual Review of Psychology*, 55: 591–621.

the extent that it involves an active request to accommodate other people's action to her will. Third, *the definition of political action does not include the means by which compliance is sought.* Punishment and rewards, ideas and convictions, empathy, compassion, solidarity, authority symbols, manipulation techniques and so on can all be instruments to achieve compliance. To define nuclear political action it is not necessary to identify the resources on which the hope of compliance is based, such as the eight values referred to by Lasswell and Kaplan (respect, moral standing, affection, well-being, skill, wealth, enlightenment and power),[27] or the sources of influence mentioned by Parsons (threats and coercion; promises, rewards or inducements; persuasion through the use of arguments or propaganda; and activation of commitments by appealing to norms).[28] Fourth, *consequentiality does not define political action*. Political action aims at consequences (compliance), but its success in achieving them does not define it. An action does not need to be effective to be political. It is obvious that lot of requests for compliance remain unanswered, are explicitly ignored or, perhaps, remain unperceived by the recipient. The success of a political action depends on other additional external conditions affecting both the requester and the sought-after.

Intentionality and compliance instigation adequately and sufficiently define political action. Political action is intentional action oriented towards affecting the behaviour of other humans in the direction of our will. I therefore provisionally state that any action implying a request for behavioural compliance is political action. Any action lacking this quality is non-political. To differentiate varieties of political action we need further elaborations, but the nucleus of a compliance search is the fixed core.

Objections

I can see three challenging objections to this position. Here I will discuss and reject the first two. The third cannot be rejected but must be answered, which will be the task of chapters 3 and 4.

The first objection to this view of nuclear political action is that seeking the compliance of others is not an independent motivation. There are other motives for seeking compliance. These are the previously mentioned morality, utility and honour motives. In other words, behavioural compliance is a 'means' to other goals, an instrument, not an autonomous and independent motivation.

This view underscores the possibility that the search for the compliance of others is a self-satisfying goal. The satisfaction of a command is similar to the

---

27. Lasswell and Kaplan, *Power and Society*.
28. Parsons, T. (1963), 'On the Concept of Influence', *Public Opinion*, 27: 37–62.

satisfaction of material interest, honour or morality. People like to command, give orders and coordinate others as much as they like to avoid sanctions, to buy goods and to be respected by their friends. Having command over others gives happiness, and one may even be able to make sacrifices on other dimensions to acquire and maintain such a desired good (as happens with all other behavioural criteria). In this case, compliance may be regarded as a desired good as much as a luxury yacht or an impeccable reputation. In addition, unless one admits a Maslowian hierarchy of needs and desires ordered in terms of priority of satisfaction, the same question applies to all other motivations. Why do we search for material rewards, honour or morality? Are they ends or means to other satisfying aims? Weber analysed the specific circumstances in which a strong inclination to acquire material rewards is *motivated* by a desire to achieve explicit signs of salvation,[29] and similar means/end loops can be recorded for all types of actions.

Curiously, the lust for command is a current theme in Western political thought and historiography, but it does not figure prominently in recent political science approaches. The Bible records a wider set of motivations from many of its characters that we contemporarily accept, although we usually see them as 'hungers' that eventually consumed and destroyed those characters' carriers. It reports David's hunger for Bathsheba, Joab's hunger for position, Gehazi's greed for Naaman's gifts, Simon's unnatural desire for the Holy Spirit, Judas's betrayal of Christ for thirty pieces of silver *and* Jezebel's lust for power. Tacitus resorts to this motivation very frequently in his *Annals of Imperial Rome*. He suggests that 'the motive of Octavian, the future Augustus, was lust for power'; that Lucius Marcus Sejanus (a hatchet man for the emperor Tiberius) 'concealed behind a carefully modest exterior an unbounded lust for power'; and that 'Drusus Caesar's degraded character was animated by power-lust'. Edward Gibbon in his *The Decline and Fall of the Roman Empire* argues that 'Of all our passions and appetites, the love of power is of the most imperious and unsociable nature, since the pride of one man requires the submission of the multitude'. Edward Wortley Montague presented an analysis of the lust for power in *Reflections on the Rise and Fall of the Ancient Republics Adapted to the Present State of Great Britain* (1759). In *Machiavellism: The Doctrine of Raison d'État and Its Place in Modern History* (English translation, 1957), Friedrich Meinecke claims that 'the striving for power is an aboriginal human impulse, perhaps even an animal

---

29. In his study of the relationship between the ethics of ascetic Protestantism and the emergence of the spirit of modern capitalism, originally published as a series of articles between 1904 and 1905 in the *Archiv für Sozialwissenschaften und Sozialpolitik* and later put together as Weber, Max (1934), *Die protestantische Ethik und der Geist des Kapitalismus*, Tübingen: J.C.B. Moh, First English edition (1930), *The Protestant Ethics and the Spirit of Capitalism*, London: Allen and Unwin.

impulse, which blindly snatches at everything around until it comes up against some external barriers. And, in the case of men at least, the impulse is not restricted solely to what is directly necessary for life and health. Man takes a wholehearted pleasure in power itself and, through it, in himself and his heightened personality'.[30]

In all these quotations, the hunger for command, although acknowledged as a motivation, follows somehow in the negative biblical footsteps. The ambition for command is always presented in derogatory terms, as a perverted or depraved appetite and, in any case, as a motivation that leads to self-destruction. This is perhaps an explanation why this ambition and desire is not seen as an honourable end in itself but rather as a dishonourable means to other final values. It is surprising to note, nonetheless, that the lust for command has received relatively little attention as a motivational drive in political science and even less attention as a defining core or nucleus of political action. Even Lasswell, the author who has perhaps most explicitly focused on power motivations and personality traits, has tended to see the search for command, which he associates with an 'accentuated power' personality, as a sort of psychopathology: 'Our key hypothesis about the power-seeker is that he pursues power as a means of compensation against deprivation'; 'the accentuation of power, we have suggested, is compensation against estimates of the self as weak, contemptible, immoral, unloved'.[31] The social psychology literature often (but not always) includes power in a rather generic sense (a desire not only to control others but also to win arguments, to enjoy respect and reputation, to like competition and winning) among personality 'needs', which is not our line of reasoning in this context.[32] Therefore, the relatively little that we have in this direction tends to see this appetite for command as a feature of disturbed personalities (such as the criminal leadership of the Stalins and Hitlers of this world), as a sort of pathological deviation. The famous rather vulgar Sicilian saying *Cumannari è megghiu di futtire* – which in a translation of attenuated vulgarity reads 'to rule is more enjoyable than making love' – recognises the independence and strength of the motivation, but in all Italian dictionaries the sentence is always presented in negative terms as signifying 'behaviours not always acceptable and to be appreciated'. And yet one wonders why we should not look at the formation of a social movement, at the internal disputes in every political organisation, at the policy outputs of

---

30. I draw these few references from the very learned Smith, George H. (2014), *The Lust for Power*, 17 January, www.libertarianism.org/columns/lust-power.

31. Lasswell, H. (1948), *Power and Personality*, New York: W. W. Norton & Company, p. 39 and p. 221, respectively.

32. For a forerunner of this view, see McClelland, D. (1961), *The Achieving Society*, Princeton, NJ: D. van Nostrand Co., which includes the 'need for power' together with the need for achievement and the need for affiliation in a theory of psychological motivations.

every government or leadership as driven by the fundamental lust for command of the individuals fostering or opposing them, and why we instead seek more 'honourable' motivations.[33]

A second objection focuses on the request for compliance as the defining feature of 'political action'. The objection claims that interest-, honour- and morality-based behaviours *also* generate requests for behavioural compliance. The latter, rather than being a motivation in itself, as argued here, may characterise other motivational bases such as interest, honour and morality. If this is the case, then a request for compliance cannot be the distinctive feature of political behaviour but it is rather a feature that is, or may be, embodied in any type of motivated action.

First, let us note that this objection does not refer to the general point of having consequences for others. Undeniably, following a code of honour may entail consequences for others in the sense of leading them to suffer the consequences of that code-based behaviour. These consequences are not intentional for the actor and therefore do not qualify his action as political; no more than unintentional consequences would qualify an action as moral. The objection suggests that actions driven by utility, honour and moral motivations may also imply a request for behavioural compliance *intentionally* addressed to other human beings. In this case, the category that I have assumed to define political action is associated with interest-, moral- and honour-motivated actions. As such, it could not be an efficient definition of nuclear political action.

Without doubt, a father can impose a code of honourable conduct on relatives such as a son or a daughter; he may require others to show respect in concrete behavioural manners. In other words, social norms may not only dictate individual behaviours but also foresee the request for others to behave according to such norms. Similarly, morally motivated behaviour may generate a request for compliance over the others, as, for instance, when you publicly object on moral grounds to others' behaviours regarded as 'immoral' or 'unethical'. You may be an honourable person behaving ethically in every circumstance without caring about the consequences of your actions. But you could also be a 'moral activist' who, on moral grounds, asks others to change their behaviour, actively engaging in denouncing and opposing other people's behaviours that do not conform to your standards. In this latter case,

---

33. Incidentally, the recognition of lust for command among the motivations for action helps to solve a host of apparently unsolvable collective action problems. Political entrepreneurs with an action motivation for command easily bear the cost of mobilising. Every organisation, even the more tenuous, foresees a large set of command, subcommand and sub-subcommand roles to attract members with command ambitions. This leaves open the problem of the adhesion of other individuals with little interest in command and whose final value is some specific policy or outcome. However, this problem relates more to the degree of success of the collective action than to its emergence.

moral-motivated action may entail a request for behavioural compliance addressed to other human beings and, as such, be indistinguishable from what I have defined here as political action.

My reply to this solid objection is the following: if a behaviour oriented by your interest, morality or honour *requires* the acquisition of compliance by others, then such behaviour is not purely interest-, morality- or honour-based, but it includes a political component. 'You should not' is very near to 'you should not allow others to'. However, this subtle distinction is the key to differentiation between pure types of behavioural motivation. Motivations of a pure moral, honour and utility type are not explicitly and intentionally characterised by a request for behavioural compliance; to the extent that they are, they incorporate a dominant political motivation different (though perhaps in addition) to the other motivations. *Whenever* honour, utility or moral actions imply pressures on others to change their behaviour, then such actions incorporate a political motivation.

A scientist may abstain from making natural experiments on the bodies of other human beings on moral grounds, a doctor can object to procuring an abortion and a conscientious objector can abstain from carrying arms or doing military service. But when the conscientious objector, the doctor and the scientist engage in actually determining the behaviours of others in accordance with their codes, then they become activists for peace and disarmament, the defence of life and respect for human rights. In this case, your action is not moral action but political action to achieve the compliance of others with your moral values. Activists engage in explicit and intentional requests for behavioural compliance. Their motivation changes and becomes inherently political *to the extent that they seek values that can only be achieved through the behavioural compliance of others*. This additional motivation *is political motivation*, which is therefore, in its pure form, independent of the concrete values the actor is seeking.

Therefore, political motivation is distinct and separate from other motivations to the extent that it is substantially defined only by the desire and the need for compliance, which is independent of any other final goal or value. As I have argued earlier, the search for compliance may be a self-sustaining motivation. It can also be a search motivated by other final values of any kind. Nevertheless, in my view, whatever the final value, the *politicalness* of the action lies in the fact that it requires and explicitly aims at the behavioural compliance of other human beings. The political element is this inbuilt request to abide by, obey and comply with whatever the final goal is, be it honour, interest, morality or appetite for command.

Political action is distinctive because as it is action directed to others it requires that others modify their behaviours, orientations and goals, which is its deliberate aim. This is not the case of the other pure behavioural orientations. Interest-based behaviours do not necessarily require others to modify their goals, behaviours and so on. When you obey or violate a law or seek a material reward, there might be consequences for others, but your behaviour does not aim to achieve those consequences and you are not even interested in what consequences there might be. Utility maximisation in its economic version does not entail the behavioural compliance of others. Morality and moral-based behaviours do not have specific characteristics of exercising action towards others. Behaviours that are based on a sense of honour and aim to achieve, maintain and increase the respect of others do not necessarily manifest themselves through an explicit request for conformity directed to relevant others and do not require them to modify their behaviours and goals.

The argument here is that whenever a pursuit for utility, defence or enhancement of your honour or respect for your morality generate pressure for others to comply with your requests, then these motivations become 'political' in the sense that a political element is added to them, whereas whenever these same motivations are followed without requiring compliance by others there is no political action element.

To sum up, I conclude that (a) morality-, utility- and honour-driven actions may have consequences for others but not always and not necessarily; (b) these consequences, when they exist, are unintentional and unexpected and they are not the explicit goal of the action, and they are independent of and indifferent to the relevant others; (c) to the extent that moral-, utility- or honour-motivated behaviours explicitly aim at a direct modification of others' preferences and behaviours, they include a dominant political motivation and depart from the pure utility, morality or honour categories.

Let us provisionally make a minimal definition. Politics is the behavioural domain in which, unlike all other domains, people act with the explicit intention to achieving compliance by others. This may be regarded as a self-satisfying final objective, as a means of achieving final objectives that, in principle, can also be achieved by other means (business, prestigious professional work, sacrifice, etc.), or as a way of achieving final objectives that necessarily depend on compliance by others and that cannot be achieved without it.

I conclude this section by alluding to the third crucial objection that remains unsolved and that will need further clarification. If we ground the nuclear element of politics in a search for compliance, we are bound to conclude that all requests for compliance have a political character. Actions by man over men in this sense exist in every sphere or arena of human interaction – the workplace, the family, associative life and so on – and so far we have defined them all as political. The objection is that a model based on the aim of achieving compliance and response is too pervasive and too general to properly circumscribe the realm of the political. This is the objection that has already been made against the 'power approach' *à la* Lasswell and which, in my view, is not properly solved in his work. It is necessary to provide a solution that differentiates among instigation/response conditions and qualifies their different degrees of politicalness. This is a core goal of this book: to provide a framework that manages to differentiate among diverse forms of compliance attempts and qualifies them according to their varying degrees of politicalness. Chapters 3 and 4 attempt this task. First, however, I need to further elaborate on the concept of behavioural compliance that I have introduced.

Behavioural compliance and power

In discussing a definition of elementary political action, I have avoided resorting to the concept of 'power'. By doing so I depart from a predominant approach, and this needs some further consideration. I regard the concept of 'power' as quite unsuitable for a characterisation of nuclear political action. First, the concept carries different meanings and connotations, most of which are 'structural' or 'systemic' rather than individual and behavioural.[34] In the Marxist conception, power is seen as a structurally determined dominant position of a social group, which translates its invisibility into a false consciousness of individuals and groups. Gramsci conceives power as a 'cultural hegemony' that allows a manufacturing of consent to the capitalist order.[35] Talcott Parsons views power as a collective facility, as power to generate some shared ends and, therefore, something all parties benefit from.[36] Niklas Luhmann goes further in this direction by objecting to the very idea of 'power asymmetry' in a group and viewing power at the systemic level as an instrument for pursuing collective goals, as a medium analogous to money.[37] Foucault – to the extent that one can reconstruct a positive definition from the many references by this author to what power is not – always views power as a structural expression of a given social relationship; it is dispersed, unlikely to be detected and elusive to investigation.[38] The analyses by these

---

34. See the anthology of meanings and conceptions of power edited in Lukes, S. (1986), *Power*, Oxford: Blackwell Publishers.
35. Gramsci, Antonio (1971), *Selections from the Prison Notebooks of Antonio Gramsci*, New York: International Publishers (1948–1951, *Quaderni del carcere*, edited by F. Platone, Torino: Einaudi).
36. Parsons, Talcott (1963), 'On the Concept of Political Power', *Proceedings of the American Philosophical Society*, 107: 232–62.
37. Luhmann, Niklas (1969), 'Klassische Theorie del Macth: Kritik ihrer Pramissen', *Zeitschrift für Politik*, n. 16: 453–65.
38. See the 'Foreword' by Gordon, Colin (1980) to Foucault, Michel, *Power/Knowledge: Selected Interviews and Other Writings 1972–1977*, New York: Pantheon Books.

distinguished thinkers go far beyond this superficial characterisation and differ in many other respects. However, it seems to me that they all conceive of power as a systemic property that is used to identify the structural imbalances or the exchange mechanisms which prevail in a given whole society. This vision of power is essential for any grand social theory, but it is less useful if the aim is to characterise the behavioural asymmetries in dyadic relationships.

Steven Lukes tries to bridge the structural view with the behavioural one in a three-dimensional account of power.[39] In his first dimension – power as decisional capacity – power is clearly a behavioural attribute that applies to individuals to the extent that they are able to modify the behaviour of other individuals within a decision-making process. The person with power in a situation is the person who prevails in the decision-making process.[40] However, Lukes then proceeds to a criticism of this one-dimensional view of power by adding two additional dimensions: power as 'agenda setting' and power as 'ideology and false consciousness', therefore moving to a more macro level. This notable attempt to conceptualise power along several dimensions evidences the problems that arise when the same concept is applied to different levels of social interpretation.[41] I will come back to the concrete interpretative shortcoming that this multilevel use generates at a later stage of the argument (pp. 125–27).

Second, power is a distal form of 'pure potential'. The classic definition by Weber defines power as 'the chance of a man or a group of men to realise their own will in a social action even against the resistance of others who are participating in the action'.[42] This definition stresses that power (a) is a relationship among parts, not an aspect of a good which is held in a fixed quantity; (b) it is a probability of realisation, and there is no complete assurance that it will yield any expected results; and (c) it is always potential, in that it is not identified in the concrete production of its effects, but it is defined as a 'capacity' to get those effects. This means that power need not be actually exercised to produce its desired effects and that power may not have the capacity to realise its effects.[43]

---

39. Lukes, Steven (1974), *Power: A Radical View*, London: Macmillan. Note that Lukes offers a definition of power by saying that A exercises power over B when A affects B 'in a manner contrary to B's interests' (ibid., p. 37), rather than 'in a manner favourable to A's interest'.

40. Lukes, *Power*, p. 18.

41. In the additional two essays in the second edition (Palgrave 2004) of his influential book, Lukes slightly changes the language by referring to 'power as domination', which manifests itself not only through explicit coercive means, but also through unconscious mechanisms.

42. Weber, Max (1978), *Economy and Society*, Berkeley: University of California Press, p. 926.

43. In fact, use consumes power, and power, therefore, is most effective when the subject manifests its subjection without power actually being deployed. Power is most effective when it is sufficient for it to be symbolically manifested, rather than being put into action. Power can operate through past memories of its effects or through imagination of future consequences of its effects.

As a *potential* to determine or modify somebody else's behaviour, power needs to rely on a variety of resources (usually identified as the triad of economic, ideological and coercive resources), which also represent *potential* means of pressure. When we use the concept of power in connection with politics, it is understood as a *means* of doing politics and political action, and it is inextricably linked to resources. Often, in connection with coercion, power constitutes the specific instrument with which political action and politics are carried out.

However, there is an important difference between saying that the use of the specific means of power *characterises* political action and saying instead that power *motivates* political action. If power is a specific means of political action, we are simply identifying potential resources brought to bear on certain kinds of intersubjective relationships. If, on the other hand, power and the search for power motivate nuclear political action, we fall more easily into the psychopathological view of political action as primarily dominated by the 'hunger for power' in its most derogatory meaning that we discussed earlier. Lust for power can motivate political action, but the latter is not reducible to it. In my view, a search for compliance motivates political action more clearly than a search for power (i.e., the accumulation of a potential capacity).

Moreover, for power to transform itself from 'potential' to 'actual' we need to add a *propensity* to use power resources and an *ability* of the actor to do so. If we see power as the essence of political action,[44] we assume that every power based on resources has the propensity to use the resources and the skill and ability to do so. From a behavioural point of view, resources, the propensity to use them and skill in using them all contribute to the existence of power *and* its successful use, but it is going too far to define nuclear political action in this way. In this sense, power points to a 'potential' that subtends to any specific political action and to the underlying resources on which may depend the likelihood of success of its deployment. Resources and the propensity and ability to deploy them all merge in the idea of power.

There cannot be a (potential) power without the resources and the propensity/ability to use them. A resourceless/propensityless/abilityless power is a non-power. On the contrary, there can be a request for behavioural compliance without the backing of resources/propensity/ability, or with insufficient or inadequate backing by them (whatever its chance of success). Power, therefore, is inextricably linked to the resources it may bring to bear on the request. Power is best characterised as the likelihood that a specific instigation is met with a positive answer. To use power as a defining property of political action (in either the presence or absence of conflict) would conflate

---

44. This is the position to which Mario Stoppino adheres.

a request for compliance with its resources and with its effectiveness. We can say that an instigation will have more chance of meeting a positive attitude the greater the power resources/propensity/ability of the petitioner. However, this statement does not define nuclear political action but rather points to the conditions for it to be effective. From the point of view of the actor, the concept of power confuses the potential resources or means (the sources of power) with its use (a request for compliance). Therefore, it is difficult to define nuclear political action using this term.[45]

Rather than focusing on the existence of a resource/propensity/ability-dependent potential, I find it preferable to focus on a more empirical aspect of the request for compliance. A concrete instigation is not potential; it is actual, even if its degree of success depends on other circumstances. Instigations can be advanced even in the absence of (power) resources. In the definition of elementary political action, the request for behavioural compliance should be seen first in its naked form, not through the resources of the actor, his propensity to use them or his ability to use them. The naked request for behavioural compliance – an intentional instigation – is enough for a *nuclear* definition. This pure form neither confuses nor conflates together several dimensions, as the concept of power does.

To sum up, I start with a blind or naked instigation and afterwards I will elaborate on the conditions for it to take different forms and different levels of politicalness. My starting point is that every request for behavioural compliance in every field – even a request for help from a close friend – is intrinsically political *from the motivational point of view*. It goes without saying that we intuitively perceive differences between a request for compliance addressed to our friends, one addressed to an associate in a business enterprise, one addressed to a political adversary in a tough decisional fight and one addressed to an entire membership group from an authority position.

---

45. An example used by Warren is telling from this point of view. If I argue with a friend about something, and we walk away without fear of retaliation or imposition, there is conflict but no power and therefore no politics. Alternatively, we could resolve the conflict through means such as talk and mutual adjustment, which are also non-political. On the contrary, if in a quarrel with my spouse about exactly the same thing I threaten divorce and to take away money, I use a dominant power position and this is political. Power appears here as a request for behavioural compliance backed by powerful resources. Warren states that 'what is at issue is whether parties seek, using their resources, to make decisions, rules, organisations, or collective action binding upon others'. Warren, Mark E. (1999), 'What Is Political?', *Journal of Theoretical Politics*, 11: 207–31. Note that in this example the term 'power' covers both the search for compliance by the spouse and the search for binding decisions over the entire membership of a field. 'Power' is directed towards another actor in the first case, and in the second case it is directed towards the monopolistic provider of behavioural compliance for the entire field, avoiding direct conflict with other actors. The power (resources) directly bearing on your spouse is not the same power (resources) bearing on the ruler. The actor you address and your resource potential are definitely different. The lowest common denominator in the two situations is a request for compliance, not power backed by resources. See pp. 110–15 for further clarification of this point.

What actually differentiates these disparate requests for compliance? What make us perceive them as inherently different? My point is that all these actions are unified by the element of a compliance search – and that is why they can all be defined as 'political' to begin with – but they are differentiated by something else. What changes are the conditions of the actors in which such a request takes place, the backing resources available, whether the instigation is occasional or stabilised over time, its level of generality with respect to the membership group and finally its degree of effectiveness? The remainder of this chapter and chapters 3 and 4 will elaborate on this differentiation, while insisting that the element unifying the political is the search for compliance by other humans.

NUCLEAR POLITICAL ACTION

The works by Harold Lasswell and Bertrand de Jouvenel that I have cited have greatly influenced my centring the definition of nuclear political action on an intentional search for compliance. The views of these two authors merit a more extended review. Both Lasswell and de Jouvenel focus on political action (which I have re-labelled 'nuclear' or 'elementary') rather than on politics in general. De Jouvenel introduces the crucial concept of 'incitement' or 'instigation' as an explicit request addressed to an individual B by another individual A taking the form of an order, a directive or also a demand or petition. Lasswell uses the concept of power to indicate the general field of study and operation of politics, while de Jouvenel uses the concept of power, in its meaning of 'instigation and response', to indicate the elementary aspects of politics.[46] According to de Jouvenel, instigation/response relationships are 'political' even when they take place in spheres usually not regarded as political. According to Lasswell, 'power relationships' share the same property. Lasswell and de Jouvenel redefine the political in different and broader ways to make it consistent with their own approaches. In doing so they both challenge the conventional definition of the political. De Jouvenel further states that what we usually and conventionally consider 'political' is only a development of the fundamental relationships that emerge in a natural way whenever humans in aggregates have the opportunity to act over one another.[47]

---

46. For a critical analysis of de Jouvenel's work in connection with that of Lasswell, see Stoppino, M. (2001), *Potere e teoria politica*, Milano: Giuffré, pp. 208–13.
47. 'We are in the presence of politics whenever a project calls for the favourable disposition of other wills, and insofar as the agent applies himself to enrol these wills'. 'any action tending to rally and enrol foreign wills is political in form'. de Jouvenel, Bertrand (1954; 1992), 'The Nature of Politics', in Dennis Hale and Marc Landy (eds.), *The Nature of Politics: Selected Essays of Bertrand de Jouvenel*, New Brunswick, NJ: Transaction, pp. 67–83, esp. 69.

He believes that the conventional understanding of politics is the result of an accentuation, systematisation and polarisation of normal social practices. In his view, political action is the capacity of man to move man, and as this phenomenon happens everywhere in society he admits that a large section of such activity is not normally considered political. He nevertheless believes that it is possible to improve our understanding of what we normally call politics by starting from elementary political action. He wants to eventually demonstrate that this definition of political action is the best way to characterise those phenomena that are conventionally located in the domain of politics.

De Jouvenel's argument develops as follows. In every group of humans that are in a set of interdependent relationships, there are several instigations. These instigations can be contradictory or compatible. If they are contradictory, they can be so only at the level of the individual or at the level of the group. If the instigations are contradictory at the level of the individual (in the sense that each individual can respond only to a single instigation but not to two) but not at the level of the group, then there is no problem as different subsets of membership of the group can follow one instigation while others follow another without this having negative consequences for the group. Two (or more) instigations are contradictory at the level of the group if the fact that some individuals respond positively to one instigation while others respond to the second destroys the group.[48]

To avoid the disintegration of the group, there are usually procedures in which only one instigation is chosen, which becomes compulsory and binding for all the members of the group. De Jouvenel labels this procedure with the outlandish term *law of conservative exclusion*.[49] This law operates as a process of selection among different instigations and provides for one instigation to be proclaimed a 'command'. There is then no liberty to propose instigations contradictory to the command. Instigation/response relationships within a group in which contradictory instigations are impossible or not allowed more clearly resemble what we consider politics in its usual and familiar sense. However, note that de Jouvenel presents this more familiar version as a specific case of the general instigation/response genus. The law of conservative exclusion constitutes a necessary condition for the persistence of a political body. This idea permits de Jouvenel to link the general theory of instigation/response (ubiquitous in the social system) to the forms

---

48. We could also use the label *competing* for those instigations to which each individual can respond positively to either without jeopardising the group and the continued relationship, and the label *conflicting* for those instigations where the group cannot survive without collectively adhering to either one or the other. To avoid a proliferation of terms, it is perhaps better to stick with the ideas of instigations that are contradictory only at the level of the individual and those which are also contradictory at the level of the group.

49. De Jouvenel, B. (1963), *The Pure Theory of Politics*, pp. 111–12.

of instigation/response that are specific to those groups for which the law of conservative exclusion applies. In so doing, he distinguishes the general category of instigation/response from its political variant.

By cleverly combining instigation/response and the law of conservative exclusion, de Jouvenel links a definition of nuclear political action with the specific conditions in which it determines the forms of what we conventionally define as political. In politics, the priority of the group is guaranteed, and contradictory instigations are excluded; in what we conventionally do not call politics, the priority of the group is not, or is less often, guaranteed, and individuals can more easily follow contradictory instigations that jeopardise the group. This conclusion makes a crucial step in the direction of linking a general definition of political action (instigation/response) to the more specific political character that can distinguish it from the large variety of such instigations in everyday life that we find difficult to characterise as political. In this way, de Jouvenel goes far beyond Lasswell's simple acknowledgement that every power relationship is political in itself. Nevertheless, this important step is not fully satisfactory on two grounds.

The first criticism is that although de Jouvenel can satisfactorily argue that the law of conservative exclusion qualifies the political character of the instigation/response, he cannot demonstrate that this is particular to politics. In fact, the law of conservative exclusion concerns not only what we usually understand as 'political communities' but also any other type of stable association, organisation or social group.[50] The binding nature of an instigation resulting from the law of conservative exclusion is not specific or unique to politics as understood in conventional terms. It also applies to voluntary associations, for instance, or to firms. Even in these cases, a process of selection must solve contradictory instigations if the entity is to persist. De Jouvenel identifies a characteristic that is typical of politics as conventionally understood but not exclusively reserved to it. His reasoning eventually leads to the conclusion that there is politics whenever there is a structure of authority, either public or private.[51] He fails, in my view, to conceptualise the element that differentiates private from public authority.

The second criticism is that there are other interaction situations among actors to distinguish. There is not only a difference between public and private bodies (which both enjoy the presence of a structure of authority), but there is also a difference between these and other fields of interactions among actors that are not characterised by the presence of a structure of authority of some type and that are nevertheless characterised by different possibilities

---

50. Stoppino, *Potere e teoria politica*, p. 216.
51. This is a position very similar to the one put forward by Eckstein, which was mentioned earlier in chapter 1, footnote 53.

of escaping from instigation/response. Even in those situations in which the law of conservative exclusion does not apply – and there is therefore no monopolistic provision of behavioural compliance – actors find themselves in different situations of potential exit.

To cut short a discussion that will be at the core of chapters 3 and 4, the work by de Jouvenel perfectly captures the dimension of a presence (or absence) of monopolisation of behavioural compliance (the law of conservative exclusion) but fails to further differentiate among interaction contexts on the dimension of the costs of exit for the actors involved. Had he operated this additional distinction, I believe he would have greatly improved his characterisation of politics as conventionally understood from other varieties of instigation/response. A more precise discussion of types of compliance request in their analytical forms is necessary. This is the task of the final section of this chapter. Subsequently, I will qualify this analytical framework in connection with different fields of human interaction in chapters 3 and 4.

Instigations and their effects on B

That political action is action whose aim is for A to move B to do X is a simple statement. Its simplicity is apparent, however. We only observe that A asks B to do X. In this form, the instigation/response based on the search for compliance is an empty form or model, and at this stage we should not read more into it than is implied. The response could in fact depend on A. A could act because he occupies a position (of authority) attached to which there is a recognised claim for compliance. A could put into the balance some accumulated personal past propensity to comply that is simply reiterated over time, based on credit, reputation or prestige and without much ad hoc evaluation. A could directly employ resources that are crucial for B and that B is oriented towards exchanging for compliance. Eventually, A could simply threaten punishment. Similarly, the motivations for B to comply do not enter the empty form. It does not discuss whether compliance by B is based on B's calculations of rewards and interest, on fear of A retaliating or reacting, on previous commitments consequent to B's promises like contracts or oaths or other forms of loyalty or on B having an affective or friendly relationship with A that gives him a positive attitude towards acquiescence. Finally, the response could also depend on X, the action required. B could like it anyway and independently of A and, in this case, the relationship is a relationship of coordination or cooperation. The combination of these elements can make investigation of the conditions for a favourable reception of the request for compliance more realistic.

As argued before, a focus on the resources used by any actor A to achieve the compliance of any actor B is not crucial in my discussion at this stage. It is more important to see the concrete *effect on B* of these potential resources.[52] From this point of view, one needs to first distinguish between explicit and non-explicit requests for compliance. *Explicit requests* for compliance refer to situations in which A does not try to hide his instigation from B and B is aware that he is the object of the request from A. *Non-explicit requests* for compliance refer to situations in which A effectively hides his instigation from B, and B is therefore not aware of the request embedded in A's action. A third possible case is that in which A does not make any request explicit, but B is aware of A's preference and may anticipate the consequence of violating the implicit request. I will deal with this under the heading of *anticipated reactions*.

Explicit requests for compliance can affect B by

(a) generating direct rewards or threats of punishment for B (*sanctions*);
(b) altering B's factual knowledge and value beliefs (*persuasion*).

The distinction between *sanctions* and *persuasion* – much like that between *conditioning* and *manipulation* which will be made later – does not refer to a substantive definition of the resources (e.g., money, coercion, oratory, gifts) controlled by A but rather to the effects they have on B.

Sanctions

Sanctions intervene in actor B's behavioural alternatives by modifying the cost-benefit analysis on which she bases her choice of conduct to follow. It is important to underline that sanctions do not change her knowledge or beliefs. Instead, they directly introduce new elements such as promises of rewards or threats of punishment that modify the relative value of each individual behavioural alternative for B. The aim is to change B's calculations.

Positive and negative sanctions, reward versus constriction or increasing returns and declining costs versus declining returns and rising costs operate very differently. Rewards increase the benefits of one course of action – the one desired by A – as compared with the other alternatives for B. Constrictions operate through an increase in the costs (the threat of a punishment) to B of all the alternatives not desired by A. The first operate with a promise of

---

52. Mario Stoppino, in *Potere e teoria politica*, pp. 133–62, provides an elaborate classification of what he calls 'forms of power'. In my opinion, he deals more with the effects of power. I have adapted his analysis to my framework and terminology. In particular, Stoppino always distinguishes between 'intentional' and 'interested' forms of power and he therefore builds (pp. 148–49) a complex taxonomy of the forms of power based on open/hidden and intentional/interested categories. I have not retained this taxonomic distinction. I have also eliminated some of his forms and added others which are more useful in my treatment. Nevertheless, in this section I remain indebted to his very perceptive treatment of the matter.

a reward for the desired behaviour; the second operate with a threat of a cost for *all* undesired behaviours.[53]

This is not a marginal difference. Negative incentives have an advantage over positive ones: while a positive incentive, a promise to reward a behaviour, must be kept, threats that are successful in influencing somebody else's behaviour do not need to be carried out. In the first case, if the request for conformity is successful, the rewards have to be delivered. They are expensive and tend to consume and exhaust when they are used. In contrast, threats of punishment do not necessarily need enforcement. If actor B follows the desired behavioural option after considering the threat of sanctions, he requires no further incitement beyond avoidance of the possible costs. However, threats are also problematic. They are cheaper for A if they are effective but face a problem of certainty and credibility if they have to be enforced. Severe deprivation threats and the actual implementation of them via explicit losses may generate strong reactions of hostility. The threat itself may feed resistance and disobedience, even if it would be better for the actor to accept the imposition and to give up. There might be a perception of risk of annihilation or destruction, which is likely to generate the most expensive resistance and to mobilise resources previously not available in the pre-threat situation.

If this is so, the threats and capacity to damage must rely on some general rule accepted as 'legitimate' by the overall field. This would normally entail a compliance claim based on a restricted domain of intervention and a defined limited scope. The result is the expectation that compliance claims should not be resisted and should be accepted by the actors who are the object of them. Put differently, to be effective, the expectation of sanctions must be supported by generally shared legitimacy beliefs that include a duty to accept or to comply with decisions that the actor has not contributed to and that (even if he has contributed to them) do not satisfy his preference. This leads to the conclusion that what matters for legitimacy is not the affected actor's actual perception or preference but instead a perception that the wider group of which she is part must respect and obey rules or orders. 'The strongest [man] is never strong enough to be always master, unless he transforms strength into right, and obedience into duty'.[54] This is the general aim of all those who claim compliance, but it only applies in special fields of relationships, as we will see in chapter 4.

---

53. See Scharpf, Fritz W. (1997), *Games Real Actors Play. Actor-Centered Institutionalism in Policy Research*, Boulder, CO: Westview Press, pp. 152–53; and Stoppino, *Potere e teoria politica*, p. 151.

54. Rousseau, Jean Jacques (1761), *The Social Contract and Discourses*, London: J.M. Dent & Sons, Book I, Chapter III, 'The Right of the Strongest'.

Persuasion

While sanctions operate through changes to behavioural alternatives, persuasion is a form of compliance search that operates by modifying the factual knowledge and/or the value beliefs of actor B. It is the process of convincing B to change his factual or value perceptions. This operates through arguments and discourses that do not include threats of punishments or promises of rewards. The symbolic elaboration of these arguments may be more or less sophisticated or well articulated, and there is no need here to enter a detailed discussion. By persuasion, I mean a direct and intentional attempt to obtain behavioural compliance, not a generic role of ideas in any social grouping. Although they are analytically distinct, there is of course a certain ambivalence between persuasion and sanctions. Messages and requests for compliance can ambiguously mix elements of both.

Implicit requests are situations in which the instigation is not explicit, and it takes a hidden form. To the extent that these requests are not openly addressed, B is not aware of them. They can affect B by

(a) adjusting B's environmental situation (*conditioning*);
(b) fiddling B's perception of the environmental situation (*manipulation*).

Conditioning

Conditioning is a form of compliance generation that intentionally operates not directly on B but on B's environmental situation. The intervention does not alter the behavioural alternatives open to B (as sanctions do) or B's beliefs and factual knowledge (as persuasion does). Conditioning operates through the distribution of resources, the dispositions to act and the values and beliefs of the configuration of actors *relevant to B*.[55] This means that conditioning intervenes in a long chain of factors. There has to be an intentional change in the environmental conditions. This change must change the factual or belief orientation of B, and this eventually has to change his perception of the behavioural alternatives. It is a long chain that leads to a weak and uncertain impact. Actors may have different propensities to react to environmental conditioning. However, we should not underestimate the indirect and long-chain character of conditioning given the degree to which humans depend on their social environment.

Manipulation

We can quickly deal with manipulation, which usually remains outside the research interest of the political scientist, as it is difficult and rare in complex

---

55. Stoppino, *Potere e teoria politica*, pp. 158–60.

and differentiated social environments. Manipulation instruments aim to change the behaviour of others through underhanded, deceptive or even abusive tactics. Psychological manipulation regularly operates on unconscious mechanisms. These methods advance the interest of the manipulator usually by exploiting weaknesses and vulnerabilities of the manipulated actor through seduction, blame projection, feigning innocence, vilification, intimidation, guilt creation and many other instruments that psychologists have studied at length.[56]

Note the appearance of a large grey area of overlap between persuasion and manipulation. In many cases, it is hard to say whether the final compliance arrived at was the result of proper persuasion or devious manipulation. In my framework, however, this empirical evaluation problem can be largely, if not totally, overcome by underlining that persuasion relates to an open and overt instigation, while in manipulative attempts the request for compliance is undeclared, if not deliberately hidden.

Anticipated reactions

Instigations not openly formulated by A and yet clearly perceived by B constitute a distinct residual case. B is aware of a request advanced non-explicitly. B could therefore behave in the way desired by A without A having explicitly required her to do so. B knows that unless she does or does not do something, A will be upset and may at a later stage use explicit instigations to seek the non-achieved compliance. This case opens up the complex domain of *anticipated reactions*, of compliance anticipated in the absence of a clear instigation. Anticipated reactions involve a problem that is crucial in any dealing with political phenomena and has given rise to considerable controversies in the literature on power and influence.[57] Anticipated reactions depend on expected rewards and compulsion; they obviously cannot depend on expected persuasion. Unlike manipulation, anticipated reactions are likely to be frequent. In more consolidated and structured relationships, compliance requests very often follow the line of reciprocal stabilised expectations. This is particularly so in all those circumstances in which the instigation/response relationship between two actors is stable over time and reaffirms itself in

---

56. See Simon, George K (1996), *In Sheep's Clothing: Understanding and Dealing with Manipulative People*, Little Rock, AR: Parkhurst Brother Publishers; and Birch, Adelyn (2015), *30 Covert Emotional Manipulation Tactics: How Manipulators Take Control in Personal Relationships*, Createspace.

57. The classic formulation of the 'law of anticipated reactions' is in Friedrich, C.J. (1937), *Constitutional Government and Politics; Nature and Development*, New York: Harper. See also the two articles by Bachrach, P. and M. Baratz (1962), 'The Two Faces of Power', *American Political Science Review*, 56: 947–52; and Bachrach, P. and M. Baratz (1963), 'Decisions and Non-Decisions: An Analytical Framework', *American Political Science Review*, 57: 632–42.

repeated circumstances, that is, whenever compliance is not a mere punctuated outcome.

Anticipated reactions generate an objection to the definition of political action as an action that embodies a request for behavioural compliance. In fact, acknowledgement of them was also a major objection to all analyses resorting to the concept of power. The presence of responses in the absence of open instigations makes it difficult to differentiate spontaneous adhesion from compliance responses.

Note that there is the possibility of reading anticipated reactions in connection with all the approaches discussed earlier that deal with power at the systemic level. The 'structural power' of groups whose positions cannot be disregarded in the productive, social or political domains is often defined exactly by them being objects of positive decisions or non-decisions that are not explicitly advocated or requested. I admit that in this case focusing on power and power resources as 'potentials' rather than on requests for behavioural compliance as 'actuals' has an advantage. In fact, by abandoning the individualistic perspective privileged so far, we may engage in a search for and analysis of structurally privileged groups whose potential power resources are such that they do not need to advance explicit requests for compliance. This approach, however, inevitably remains in the relatively rarefied domain of power, of potential, and depends either on systemic, functional or reputational mechanisms to identify and measure such powers in the absence of explicit manifestations of it. In certain situations, this is the only option available. The power that is so powerful that it does not need to manifest itself through instigations is almost invisible.

Nonetheless, the momentous problem of anticipated reactions should not convince us to renounce the considerable advantages of a motivational definition of political action. Motivation remains the distinctive element, even if it is difficult to identify the instigation. To limit the ravaging impact of anticipated reactions, it can be argued that even groups and individuals who seek compliance without asking for it explicitly must feed a process of providing explicit information about their preferences and must at some stage have proven their capacities to sanction, persuade or condition. That is, anticipated reactions probably rest on at least some prior experiences of the expected reactions. Anticipated reactions imply something that exists independently of explicit requests for compliance, but at one time or another that must have spread, and with some regularity, information about or examples of the explicit content of the implicit requests. In the total absence of these examples and proofs, evidence of these unexpressed requests will manifest only itself when the negative consequences of violating them emerge. Nevertheless, it is hard to believe that such actors would wait for the negative effects of their implicit claims to be disregarded before making them explicit.

CONCLUSION

In the final section of this chapter, I have discussed the pros and the cons of 'power-based' and 'compliance-based' definitions of nuclear political action. I have amply argued my preference for the latter. However, the two conceptions share a weakness: both are too broad categories to specify the distinctive features of the political as conventionally understood. The advantage of focusing on power in political theory lay in disentangling 'politics' from the traditional field of 'government'. However, power is evident in a large variety of different social relationships, and the power phenomenon is certainly not exclusive to that sphere of relationships usually identified with politics and the political. Making power the defining element of politics enlarges the definition of the political to the entire social process inasmuch as it is affected by power. Power as such identifies a social phenomenon which is too general and pervasive to be a theoretical object in the study of politics.

The same argument applies to requests for compliance. There is a search for compliance in a group of peers and in a tennis club, at the workplace and in an election campaign. All political relationships rest on compliance requests and production, but not all searches and requests for compliance are equally significant of the most developed and advanced configuration of the political. In defining any request for behavioural compliance as inherently political nuclear action, I offer a clear minimal definition, which definitely remains, however, very broad. I have discussed at some length the way in which de Jouvenel differentiates among the universe of instigations by distinguishing those that more closely correspond to our intuitive conception of politics from those that do not. I have criticised his conclusion while admiring the elegance of his argument. In chapters 3 and 4, I will elaborate on this problem and make my own proposal.

Awaiting this, the question is: how much agreement does this minimal definition of nuclear political action obtain? Every term is contestable in human sciences, but to consider any characterisation as a step forward we should be able to reduce and circumscribe the contestation. The contestation should focus on the peripheral terms not the core ones. A dispute about core terms is a dispute over basic forms, minimal conditions, while peripheral disputes are typically about extension. Contests over extension do not need to affect core terms and meaning. Core terms are such because they can be retained in disputes over what counts as 'politics'.[58]

A second and closely connected question is the following: is a focus on a core term (in my case 'search for compliance') consistent with the

---

58. Frohock, F.M. (1978), 'The Structure of Politics', *American Political Science Review*, 72: 859–70, esp. p. 868.

heterogeneous set of political phenomena? In other words, how much of the heterogeneous phenomenology and the descriptive scope of 'politics' as usually understood are we obliged to sacrifice with my definition of its core or elementary structure? I argue that the core term 'compliance search' is a necessary but not sufficient condition for identification of the complex phenomenology of the political. We need to engage in the clarification of more peripheral conditions that concretise different instances of the search for conformity. This may increase theoretical contestation, but provisional acceptance of the definition of the nuclear content of political action will help us follow the successive reasoning and specifications. The value of this perspective rests, therefore, on its capacity to further differentiate requests for behavioural compliance as a general category into the multifaceted varieties of it in different significant contexts. If we are looking for a nuclear definition of political action, this is probably as far as we can go.

Let us therefore sum up and anticipate the direction we will take in chapter 3. In every field of interaction, *somebody requests something*. It may be a trade union leader asking his members to support a specific action, a family member aiming to convince relatives, an associate of a voluntary organisation asking for more accountability of the leadership, a street mob protesting against something, voters at elections, lobbyists and interest groups, representatives asking high administrative officials for a hearing or terrorists killing innocent people in highly publicised actions. They *all request something*. The 'politicalness' of these acts is not in the specific value being sought (better pay, punishment of police misbehaviour, the repeal of unfriendly regulation, the liberation of comrades, etc.) but in the compliance needed to realise such values. The need for compliance on which the final values necessarily rest is what unifies all these actions and is what I call 'the political'.

Differences among requests for compliance lie in the type of interaction between A and B within which they manifest themselves. The two fundamental interaction conditions that differentiate among requests for behavioural compliance are the *level of confinement of the actors* and the *level of monopolisation of the function of behavioural compliance production*. I hope to be able to characterise the different types of request for behavioural compliance and the different intensities of their 'politicalness' in terms of specific combinations of these conditions. I aim at a theory of requests for compliance in different instigation/response environments. This is what I shall turn to in chapters 3 and 4.

Chapter 3

Conditions for political action: Confinement and monopolisation

CONFINEMENT OF ACTORS

I have argued that political action is that which is motivated by a wish to achieve the compliance of other humans with the attainment of one's own goals (including the goal of satisfaction of commanding). I now specify the conditions under which this nuclear political action acquires and displays additional properties that further qualify its 'politicalness'.

The political so understood takes its first quantum leap in conditions of precluded or highly constrained exit, which I label situations of 'confinement of actors'. This confinement is often implicit or taken for granted in discussions on politics, particularly in the many cases when they start from an existing state, political community, political system or the like.[1] States or governments are usually sources of decisions from which it is difficult or impossible to subtract, and discussion of the confinement of actors rarely goes much beyond this point. Here, I invert the argument, as I want to investigate confinement as a property of interactions between actors. In this case, confinement is not seen as a feature of specific kinds of decision but rather as a prerequisite for the *non-voluntariness of interactions* and therefore as a precondition for the manifestation of more pregnant forms of compliance.

A great deal of contemporary theorising starts from individuals (or collective actors whose constitutive conditions allow them to act strategically) and moves on to 'institutions', interpreted as sets of 'rules' (formal and informal) and to 'organisations', interpreted as sets of 'roles', along the way

---

1. Both Sartori, G. (1973), 'What Is "Politics"', *Political Theory*, 1: 5–26, and Warren, M.E. (1999), 'What Is Political?', *Journal of Theoretical Politics*, 11: 222, make only implicit reference to the no-exit situation in their discussions of the political.

overcoming possible collective action problems. The line that goes from individuals to their interactions constitutes a premature jump that leaves a number of preconditions unspecified. Considerable gains are offered by further elaborating on the conditions under which individuals are obliged to interact with other individuals and face social dilemmas – according to certain schools – or power and coercion – according to others.

Exit

Hirschman's key intuition is to conceive of exit and voice as alternative reactions by individuals to a declining performance by the organisations, institutions or situations they live in. He originally thought that exit mechanisms were typical of economic transactions, while voice mechanisms were typical of political interactions, where the usual alternative to voice is acquiescence or indifference rather than exit. Exit is impersonal; it avoids costly face-to-face relationships; it is communicated indirectly via statistics. Voice, as an attempt to change an objectionable state of affairs rather than to escape from it, is not a private or secret act but requires the expression of critical opinions through personal involvement. It is direct and visible, and it exposes the 'voicer'.[2]

Hirschman establishes a negative association between the two: opportunities for exit reduce the need or willingness for voice, while their absence enhances them. Although in later writings Hirschman increasingly appraises the role of voice, in a first approximation voice is a residual of exit. Those who do not or cannot exit are candidates for voice; voice feeds either on inelastic demand (i.e., slowness in exiting when deterioration occurs) or on lack of opportunity to exit. Therefore, the role of voice increases as the opportunity for exit declines, to the point where, 'with exit wholly unavailable, voice must carry the entire burden of alerting, management to its failing'.[3] In other

---

2. Hirschman, A.O. (1970), *Exit, Voice, and Loyalty. Responses to Decline in Firms, Organizations, and States*, Cambridge, MA: Harvard University Press, pp. 15–16 and 24. Hirschman concludes that in all organisations 'for competition to work as a mechanism of recuperation from performance lapses, it is generally best to have a mixture of *alert* and *inert* customers'. Alert customers provide information on the decline of the product, and inert customers prevent this decline from having immediate and catastrophic effects with no possibility of recovery for the firm. He also applies the same reasoning to the state: 'Every state . . . requires for its establishment and existence some limitations or *ceilings* on the extent of exit or of voice or of both. In other words, there are levels of exit (disintegration) and voice (disruption) beyond which it is impossible for an organisation to exist as an organisation. At the same time, an organisation needs *minimal* or *floor* levels of exit and voice in order to receive the necessary feedback about its performance'. Hirschman, A.O. (1981), 'Exit, Voice, and Loyalty: Further Reflections and a Survey of Recent Contributions', in A.O. Hirschman (ed.), *Essays in Trespassing. Economics to Politics and Beyond*, Cambridge: Cambridge University Press, pp. 213–35 and 224–25 (originally published in 1974 in *Social Science Information*, 13: 7–26). This line of Hirschman's reasoning is not directly relevant in this context.
3. Hirschman, *Exit, Voice, and Loyalty*, p. 34.

words, exit and voice are alternatives, and the prospect of an effective use of exit affects the resort to voice.[4] While in *Exit, Voice, and Loyalty*, Hirschman regarded exit as essentially costless when available, he later briefly discussed the potential costs of exit even in situations in which loyalty is absent.[5] Such costs, which are not evident in consumer choices, become more obvious in inter-firm transactions (trust, traditions, etc.) and are crucial in all forms of territorial exit.

However, Hirschman's main reference point is always that of individual exit opportunities *within* state organisations. In fact, he defines a 'stateless' situation as one associated with a regular practice and a possibility of physical exit, and views this as the reason for the non-emergence of large centralised societies with specialised state organs. That is, the availability of exit options prevents the formation of modern states, since the process depends on limiting these exits.[6] Even when he deals with exit from and voice for public goods, the question is whether to exit or to voice within state organisations. While exiting from an organisation providing private goods terminates the relationship, in the case of public goods the member can stop being a producer but cannot stop being a consumer. The customer who exits from public good production cannot avoid caring about their quality, as she is always subject to the need to consume them. In fact, the actor may avoid exiting to prevent further deterioration of the product quality. Hirschman is rarely concerned with other units of exit than the individual. Exits of resources or territories all imply exit from the state, something that he tends to see in the classic terms of *de-location* and *secession*.[7] 'Exit is ordinarily difficult, though not always wholly impossible, from such primordial human groupings as family, tribe, church, and state'.[8]

This brief outline highlights the great potential of Hirschman's concept and at the same time its limitations when applied outside and beyond the frame of reference of the modern territorial state, a frame that he takes for granted in his early work and only partially revises in his later studies. However,

---

4. There is some empirical evidence for the idea that people who are less likely to exit are more likely to voice. See Orbell, J.M. and T. Uno (1972), 'A Theory of Neighbourhood Problem Solving: Political Action vs. Residential Mobility', *American Political Science Review* 66: 471–89. Their results suggest that a differential distribution of exit options also has a bearing on the differential options to voice.

5. In Hirschman, 'Exit, Voice, and Loyalty: Further Reflections and a Survey of Recent Contributions', 222–23.

6. Hirschman, A.O. (1978), 'Exit, Voice and the State', *World Politics* 31: 90–107; reprinted in Hirschman, A.O. (1981), *Essays in Trespassing. Economics to Politics and Beyond*, pp. 246–65, from which I quote pp. 250–51.

7. 'The exit concept could, of course, be extended to cover cases of this sort. I shall, however, limit myself here to situations in which physical moving away of individuals or groups is an essential characteristic of the splitting up process'. Hirschman, 'Exit, Voice and the State', p. 249.

8. Hirschman, *Exit, Voice, and Loyalty*, p. 79.

with some developments and modification his conceptualisation applies in principle to any form of social interaction.

Voice is a request for behavioural compliance, while exit is the possibility of escaping from an undesired social relationship that involves possible compliance requests. The individual costs of exit vary, and therefore not all actors have the same possibilities and opportunities of exiting. This leaves open the possibility that dissatisfied mobiles – those who might exit – make the specific field of interaction particularly sensitive to their needs if preventing exit is a preference of other actors in the field. Moreover, the options open to some will probably affect those open to others, and exit choices may well provoke reactions of voice in those who do not possess or who do not want to use the option. Inequality of exit, together with its consequences, is then a possible source of conflict within a given field. In most social interactions, how much exit the field permits is a controversial issue in terms of how much control should be exercised over its membership boundaries. Unequally distributed exit options may be a basis for conflicts among those who want to restrict those options and those who want to open them up. To illustrate, the quality of schooling in suburbs is affected when the richer and most highly educated citizens leave. Not only do the schools lose the most likely vocal defenders of quality standards, but they may also lose the material resources through which a certain qualitative standard is also guaranteed to those who could not otherwise afford it.

At the abstract level, discussion of differential individual options to exit – and of the corresponding level of actor confinement – cannot progress any further. In concrete situations, specific mechanisms and techniques of boundary building define the chances of exit, which are features of the system external to individual choice. Barriers to exit (and to entry) are advocated and set at all levels in any social field and are justified on various grounds, from improving efficiency to guaranteeing professional credentials to defending useful social institutions and even to stimulating voice in deteriorating but recoverable organisations which would be prematurely destroyed by free exit. The alternatives of exit from within-state organisations, on the one hand, and migration and secession from the state, on the other hand, are too radical if we want to broaden the theoretical framework to include all forms of potential social fields from which exit is possible or not possible and more or less costly.[9] We therefore need to elaborate on boundary building, without which discussion of the confinement of actors remains too speculative. Boundaries

---

9. I have dealt more extensively with the 'cost of exit' concept in Bartolini, S. (2005), *Restructuring Europe. Centre Formation, System Building and Political Structuring between the Nation State and the EU*, Oxford: Oxford University Press, chapter 1, from which this section draws.

define the configuration of the individual actors and resources *locked in* a given social relationship field.

Boundaries

The concept of 'boundary' is the macro equivalent of the individualistic concept of 'exit'. In fact, each choice of exit (or entry, of course) always implies the transcendence of some barrier. Exit is the transfer of a component part from one system to another. At the most general level, exit is always the crossing of an established boundary, however tenuous it might be.

All potential forms of mobility bring with them a constant threat of exit, together with the development of pressures to contain movements within boundaries. The building of boundaries sets the costs and payoffs of barriers against various types of transactions across communities, membership groups, organisations and territorial entities. In this way, boundaries *lock in* crucial resources and actors within the system and determine the internal configuration of politically relevant resources. Boundaries are *locking-in mechanisms* that increase the cost of exit and set differential incentives to stay within the field.[10] These locking-in mechanisms can affect the interests of actors and corresponding instrumental calculations when they impinge on the material costs of exit/entry. They can also affect the identities of actors and their solidarities when they impinge on the cultural costs of exit. They can affect the safety and integrity of actors when they impinge on administrative, coercive and violent impositions. As a result, every strategy for differential control of boundaries has consequences for the configuration of the political resources inside each membership or territorial group. This factor deserves special attention when we deal with the forms of domestic political structuring of territorially defined communities.[11]

Boundaries, therefore, are the elements that determine the level of openness or closedness of a social relationship. This concept of boundary is not a core element in Weberian terminology, yet boundary is the key item that defines a crucial dichotomy in Weber: that between 'open' and 'closed' social relationships. A social relationship is open towards the exterior 'if and insofar as its system of orders does not deny participation to anyone who

---

10. Seeing boundaries as 'locking-in' mechanisms for individuals, resources and territories is typical of Rokkan's vision, although in his historical and empirical work he refers primarily to external territorial boundaries. See Rokkan, Stein (1999), *State Formation, Nation Building, and Mass Politics in Europe. The Theory of Stein Rokkan*, edited by Peter Flora with Stein Kuhnle and Derek Urwin, Oxford: Oxford University Press, pp. 97–107.

11. Domestic political structuring of a confined set of actors/resources is outside the scope of this book. Sketches of my way of viewing this problem can be found in Bartolini, *Restructuring Europe. Centre Formation, System Building and Political Structuring between the Nation State and the EU*, pp. 24–55.

wishes and is actually in a position to do so'. In contrast, a social relationship is closed towards the exterior 'so far as, according to its subjective meaning and its binding rules, participation of certain persons is excluded, limited or subject to restrictions'. 'If the participants expect that the admission of others will lead to an improvement of their situations, an improvement in degree, in kind, in the security or the value of the satisfaction, their interests will be in keeping the relationship open. If, on the contrary, their expectations are of improving their positions by monopolistic tactics, their interest is in a closed relationship'.[12]

By setting the level of closeness of a given social relationship, boundaries determine a clear distinction between the 'ins' and the 'outs', and this criterion of exclusion is based on unequal access to rewards, resources and opportunities, no matter what the basis for unequal access is.[13] The closure practices that derive from boundary setting can develop along various criteria: lineage, property, education, credentials, power and force, status, race, ethnicity, gender, religion, language and so on and are based on different *rules or codes of closure*. Legal apparatuses only back certain boundaries and their corresponding exclusion rules. For instance, international borders can be interpreted as a set of boundaries that close the social relationships between insiders and outsiders, to the extent that they set the distinctions and differences in membership rights, privileges and obligations between 'natives' and 'foreigners'. Similarly, even the most fragile club sets distinctions and differences in the rights, privileges and obligations of members versus non-members.

Boundaries define collectivist and individualistic criteria for exclusion and closure.[14] Collectivist criteria for exclusion are directly responsible for the transmission of advantage to other members of a group (e.g., family descendants, lineage, caste, race, ethnicity or state membership). Individualistic criteria too (property, power, credentials and achievements) are designed to protect advantages, but they are less efficient than collectivist criteria in transmitting such advantages to descendants or the next generation of group members. In Western cultures, a long-term tendency exists for individualist criteria of exclusion to replace collectivist ones.

Five features differentiate among boundaries. The *nature* of a boundary distinguishes between 'territorial' and 'functional' boundaries. In conditions

---

12. Weber, M. (1921–1922; 1978), *Economy and Society*, vol. 1, Berkeley, Los Angeles, London: University of California Press, p. 43.
13. See Murphy, R. (1988), *Social Closure. The Theory of Monopolization and Exclusion*, Oxford: Clarendon Press, p. 46 for an elaboration of the concept of 'exclusion'. Closure theory builds up from scattered elements drawn from the works of Weber and Marx.
14. For this distinction, see Parking, F. (1979), *Marxism and Class Theory. A Bourgeois Critique*, London: Tavistock.

of low socio-economic development, low technology and sense-based communication, all sorts of social interactions are land- and distance-bound; they are thus largely territorial. Changes in technology, the economy and communication foster the development of patterns of interaction and of organisations that are increasingly non-spatial. These 'functional' communities are non-spatial in the sense that they regroup people who are separated by distance and without direct face-to-face interaction. The rules, norms, principles, roles and behaviours governing identification of their members identify the boundaries of these communities.

The *type* of a boundary designates the type of input the boundary filters. Boundaries are of different types in the sense that they may filter emotional and affective relations, social rights, market interactions and economic transactions, cultural messages, administrative regulations, legal jurisdictions, credentials, lineage, property and so forth.

The *permeability* of a boundary refers to the extent to which external entries and internal exits are screened, filtered and selected. Boundaries can be open or closed, high or low and to a greater or lesser extent, where these terms indicate the degree to which external inputs can penetrate through the boundary and internal elements can exit across those same boundaries. Openness is normally associated with options and choices for the individual actor: to communicate and receive information, to know and to be known, to select one's own membership affiliation, to enter and walk out of groups and organisations. Openness has costs for systems, units and organisations, as members and resources can easily abandon them when they face competitive pressures. Similarly, even boundary closedness entails costs, as boundary control structures and agencies consume energies and resources.

Coincidence is the characteristic that refers to the level of overlapping that exists among different 'types' of boundaries. Whether different types of boundaries impinge on the same territory or membership group or, alternatively, are territorially or functionally 'disjointed' has crucial implications for the nature of the unit, system, organisation or group. Most theories of social and political structuring – such as theories of social stratification, of inter-group conflict, of political behaviour and of nation-state development – assume that the degree of coincidence or overlapping that occurs between different types of boundaries is crucial, even if they do not use the concept of boundary.

Finally, the *effectiveness* of any boundary refers to the extent to which the decision-makers in the unit/system/organisation/relationship regulate the other features of a boundary. In other words, it refers to the extent to which a central hierarchical role is able to control entries and exits by intentionally varying the degrees of permeability, coincidence and so on. This capacity depends on something that we will discuss in the next section under the heading of 'Monopolisation'.

Chapter 3

Nature, type, permeability, coincidence and *effectiveness*[15] describe features covering the variations in empirical and historical boundaries. Our daily experience and historical memory as individual members of (nation) states – a system with highly overlapping boundaries – lead us to perceive a situation of extended, if not complete, territorial overlap and coincidence of boundaries of different types. However, there is no need to do this; on the contrary, there are considerable advantages to treating the concepts of exit and boundary as theoretical categories that in principle can apply to any kind of human social relationship in any kind of historical context. Individuals are embedded in and/or enter into a variety of social relationships with other individuals: family, work, love, exchange, violence, friendship and so on. These social relationships identify distinct fields characterised by the presence of a predominant *mode of interaction* – which is either negotiation, competition, cooperation or conflict – resting on a variety of *actor orientations* such as solidarity, egotism, altruism, hostility, cooperation, self-destruction or even mutual destruction.[16]

In the perspective of this book – nuclear political action and the nature of politics – I consider the distinction that separates fields based on *the level of confinement of the actors involved in the social relationship* to be crucial. The costs of exit and the associated different levels of boundary closure determine the level of confinement. I label as *open fields*[17] those in which the actors involved in the specific social relationship are bonded together with relatively thin boundaries and therefore have the capacity and the possibility of leaving the relationship at no or very low cost. By contrast, I label as *closed fields*[18] ones

---

15. Another feature of boundaries is their *degree of importance*: the degree to which the key goal or focal activity of a system depends on the efficiency of boundary maintenance. For instance, in certain historical periods the focal activity of a territorial system can only be maintained if its military boundary is effective in screening the intrusion of an alternative military force. In different contexts or times, the ability to exclude alternative legal jurisdictions can be the crucial capacity for maintaining the system. See Strassoldo, R. and R. Bubert (1973), 'The Boundary. An Overview of Its Current Theoretical Status', in *Boundaries and Regions. Explorations in the Growth and Peace Potential of the Peripheries*, Trieste: Edizioni Lint, Proceedings of the conference 'Problems and Perspectives of Border Regions', pp. 29–57, esp. p. 49.

16. In this volume, I neither theoretically discuss the orientations of actors nor the modes of interaction that derive from them. For these, see Bartolini, S. (1999), 'Collusion, Competition and Democracy. Part I', *Journal of Theoretical Politics*, 11: 435–70; and Scharpf, Fritz W. (1997), *Games Real Actors Play. Actor-Centered Institutionalism in Policy Research*, Boulder, CO: Westview Press, pp. 84–89.

17. In resorting to the concept of 'field', I am drawn into the vast literature on 'field theory' with the idiosyncratic use of this term by many of its most representative scholars, such as Bourdieu, Pierre (1984), *Distinction: A Social Critique of the Judgment of Taste*, London: Routledge; and Bourdieu, Pierre (1993), *The Field of Cultural Production*, Cambridge: Polity Press. The reader will realise that my use of the term is less demanding and does not imply the many strings attached to it in these theories.

18. Lasswell and Kaplan (1950), *Power and Society*, p. 78 used the term 'arena' referring to closed fields for the first time but with a somewhat different meaning. Dahl, R. (1966), 'Patterns of Opposition', in Robert A. Dahl (ed.), *Political Opposition in Western Democracies*, New Haven, CT;

which are characterised by low permeability boundaries the transcendence of which entails considerable costs and in which, therefore, actors are 'confined' and find leaving the social relationship impossible. It should be understood that no social relationship is completely closed or open. The correct distinction is between the different 'costs of exit' generated by the nature, type, permeability, coincidence and effectiveness of the boundaries around the field. For present purposes, I employ the dichotomy between openness and closedness because of my interest in pure types and for analytical simplification.

If exit is possible and actors are not confined, then they can evaluate the relevance and the advantageousness of escaping from *negotiated, conflictual, competitive* or *cooperative* social relationships with others. If an actor can subtract herself from the field and the social relationship, there is no effective way of preventing the potential loser, the dissatisfied or disappointed, the wealthy or the fearful, from fleeing to a distant part of the forest. In open fields and with weak boundaries and easy exit, the possibility exists of not negotiating, cooperating, competing or conflicting and of limiting interactions to uncoordinated unilateral choices. A non-confinement of actors naturally fosters interactions that are exclusively voluntary and based on synallagmatic exchanges – bilateral or multilateral agreements in which all the parties reciprocally undertake obligations. The essence of a synallagmatic relationship lies precisely in the impossibility of one party forcing the other to accept, acquiesce or obey, and this impossibility depends on the factual and physical possibility of one of the parties subtracting herself from undesired commitments and obligations. In an open field, therefore, any attempt to generate compliance by whatever means faces the risk of the exit of those of whom compliance is requested. We can say that the 'politicalness' of a search for compliance with one's final goals and values is enfeebled if not undermined when there is the possibility of the other subtracting herself from such pressure by leaving an unappealing social relationship.

Closed fields are more interesting from the point of view of compliance production.[19] A closed field exists when actors perceive themselves to be locked into a network of mutual interactions they cannot escape from, when a certain level of interaction is compulsory and unavoidable.[20] Confinement

---

London: Yale University Press, p. 338 speaks of 'sites' of opposition, referring, however, more to sites as institutions rather than analytical types of relationship. For analytical clarity, I should perhaps reserve the term 'fields' for open ones and adopt the term 'arena' for closed fields. However, this multiplication of terms would be cumbersome, and I will therefore use 'open' and 'closed' fields.

19. See also Murphy, *Social Closure*.
20. Boudon distinguishes between two systems of interactions among actors. In 'functional systems' interactions depend on a division of labour and the actors are bound by roles pertinent to this division. In 'systems of interdependence' interactions are not based on a division of labour and the actors behave independently of each other. Boudon, R. (1979), *La logique du social*, Paris: Hachette. In systems of interactions there are roles and role expectations, and therefore internalisation of norms

deprives actors of the possibility of avoiding undesired interactions. In this context, it is not necessary to enter a detailed discussion of the causes and mechanisms involved in the circumscription of actors. Confinement of actors may be an explicit goal of some actors, or an unintended effect of scarcity or of geographical bondedness. *Environmental circumscription* may result from physical or natural barriers that confine actors. In conditions of no or low environmental circumscription, a concentration of particularly valuable resources (land, water, food, minerals, services, etc.) works in the same way, and *resource concentration* is therefore another source of circumscription. A high population density in an area can produce similar effects. It becomes difficult for people in the core central area to escape by moving away, and we may call this *population pressure circumscription*. Force and violence are means of *coercive circumscription*.[21] People, resources and territories may also be confined (or de-confined) by the attainment and maintenance (or loss) of certain rights, such as just claims or prerogatives. 'Competences', such as rewards or pay; 'faculties', such as anything that provides a basis for a claim, such as a legal right of possession; 'capacities', such as positions, functions or roles; 'titles', such as conferred powers or privileges can all be powerful sources of *social circumscription* in the sense that these prerogatives can no longer be exercised if the actor exits the social relationship. On the other hand, 'liberties', such as freedom from control, interference, restriction or obligation and right to act according to choice are significant elements of de-confinements.

A confinement of actors is, therefore, not exclusively a sort of ab initio condition that once achieved triggers the consequences mentioned here. Confinement and de-confinement of actors (resources and territories) take place constantly in history and are certainly not limited to any initial constitutive event. Confinement is constantly regenerated and fought over, even within the most consolidated territorial systems. However, 'original confinement' is often the most intriguing and mysterious process in the constitution of every human community. No other means or mechanism through which politics substantiates itself in subsequent phases can perform and legitimate this constitutive act. An act of original confinement is the metaphorical 'big bang' of politics, to which no political theory applies. The source of politics lies in a discontinuity of politics. It is certainly not based on institutions,

---

is more likely. I subsume this important distinction under the abstract label 'costs of exit', which are much higher in the latter case. This is enough for my argument here.

21. On the theory of circumscription applied to early state formation, see Carneiro, R. L. (1970), 'A Theory of the Origins of the State', *Science* 169: 733–38; Carneiro, R. L. (1978), 'Political Expansion as an Expression of the Principle of Competitive Exclusion', in R. Cohen and E. R. Service (eds.), *Origins of the State*, Philadelphia: Institute for the Study of Human Issues, pp. 205–23; Carneiro, R. L. (1988), 'The Circumscription Theory', *American Behavioural Scientist*, 31: 497–511.

none of which pre-exist the confinement. Primitive circumscriptions result from objective facts or decisions which have no authoritative basis except their own factuality. 'Such breakout entities are by nature measures, not norms. . . . Their necessity arises from the particular circumstances of an individual case, an unexpected abnormal situation. If in the interest of the whole that such renegade entities are formed, the superiority of the existential over mere normativity is apparent. Whoever authorised such acts and is capable of acting is sovereign'.[22]

In this analytical treatment, I limit myself to identifying confinement as a prerequisite for the systematic – and no longer erratic and discontinuous as in an open field – search for the behavioural compliance of others. Confinement generates a necessity of some form of interaction with others that is not chosen voluntarily. On the other hand, a search for the acquiescence of other actors which cannot leave the inescapable interactions of the field may achieve certain values and goals that are not in reach by means of unilateral action or synallagmatic exchanges. Therefore, interactions take the form of *unavoidable* competition, conflict, cooperation or negotiation relationships and trigger attempts at subjugation and domination. Phrased differently, interactions among locked-in actors *inevitably* generate forms of *action by men over other men* aimed at obtaining the compliance of the latter with the will of the former without which their final values/goals cannot be achieved. The possibility that the behavioural compliance of some can be a goal for some others, and the perception of the former that this cannot simply be avoided leads to a quantum change in the nature of political relationships. Closed fields, therefore, *generate a search for the behavioural compliance of others and a transformation of the generic possibility of political action into a necessity*. Closed fields manifest a distinctly different and greater politicalness of interactions.

The process of confinement of actors is at the root of any form of compliance production, and it is largely *about it*. In chapter 2, I argued that the political manifests itself in a project that calls for a favourable disposition of the will of others. Here, I argue that as a precondition this project requires the confinement of actors whose compliance is necessary for the project. Politics is first of all a 'confinement of actors' so that it can strengthen compliance claims towards them. 'De-confinement' of actors tends to free them from such requests and to correspondingly reduce the intensity of the political. This leads to a conceptualisation of 'compliance' as generalised and stabilised – which is predominant in closed fields – as opposed to punctuated and erratic – which is predominant in open fields (see chapter 4) and introduces the second

---

22. Schmitt, Carl (1928; 2010, 10th ed.), *Verfassungslehre*, Berlin: Duncker & Humblot, p. 107.

dimension along which different forms of compliance can be differentiated: monopolisation of command.

MONOPOLISATION OF COMMAND

Fields of interaction also differentiate themselves in terms of the extent to which the production of compliance is decentralised, scattered and occasional, as opposed to centralised, generalised (valid for all actors in the field) and stabilised over time (not time-specific or ephemeral). Fields differ according to the extent to which the production of behavioural compliance is monopolised or not, and therefore to the presence or absence of an (institutional) actor specialised in the production of compliance for the entire field. This monopolisation is a particularly mysterious process. How does it come about that within any given human group, be it a voluntary membership group or a territorial group, the command function gets to be entirely reserved to one individual or a subset of individuals through a more or less complex set of procedures and rules? How a monopolistic provider of behavioural compliance is constituted is probably the most important and foundational question for politics and political science. All of us live in situations in which this territorial monopolisation is in one way or another achieved. Those who live in situations where this is not the case most often regret the state of affairs and live with considerable uncertainty and insecurity. We very rarely have the opportunity to observe the constitution of a territorial monopoliser. Most often, we merely see the substitution of one monopoliser by a different one.

There is, of course, no need for this monopolisation to take place in any given field. Many fields are in fact without a monopolistic provider of compliance. However, when monopolisation takes place the nature of what we call politics changes radically. Monopolisation of command is the process that constitutes the loci of the 'collectivised' decisions that Sartori refers to.[23]

Monopolisation refers to situations in which groups of humans who are in a set of interdependence relationships cannot survive as a group unless one request for compliance is eventually selected as a 'command' and prevails over any other set of competing instigations. If different requests for compliance are contradictory only at the level of the individual (in the sense that each individual can respond only to a single request but not to two or many) but not at the level of the group, then there is no special problem. Different subsets of the members of the group can effectively follow one instigation while others follow other instigations without it having negative

---

23. Sartori, G. (1973), 'What Is "Politics"', *Political Theory*, 1: 5–26.

consequences for the group. If, on the contrary, the two instigations are contradictory at the level of the group, the group is weakened and destroyed by the fact that some individuals respond positively to one instigation while others respond to a different one.[24] I use the term 'monopolisation of command and of compliance production' for the outcome of the process through which only one request for behavioural compliance is chosen, which becomes compulsory and binding for all members of the group. The process of selection among different solicitations provides for one request for compliance to be proclaimed as the 'command' and strongly limits the liberty to propose instigations contradictory to it. The presence of a specialised actor or institution that monopolises the source of command similarly monopolises the source of compliance production.

If a group of friends heatedly discuss whether to go to a theatre, a pub or to see a movie in the evening, the request for behavioural compliance that extends from some members of the group to the entire group is indeed contradictory at the individual level as no one can simultaneously go to more than one place. But it is not necessarily contradictory for the group as such, as the possibility of different subgroups choosing different options does not jeopardise the friendship relationship. In contrast, if a group of lawyers heatedly discuss the professional choices of their associated law office, the group cannot survive with subgroups of individuals independently pursuing their preferred options in a specific circumstance. Either one request for compliance acquires priority over another (by whatever means or process) or the group is likely to dissipate. The social relationship on which the group is based (friendship in one case and professional cooperation in the other) can or cannot survive the presence of instigations that are contradictory at the group level. The capacity of a group bonded by some social relationship to overcome solicitations that are contradictory at the level of the group always depends on a process of monopolisation of command. This establishes a close link between the monopolisation of command and the development of political institutions. This introductory work about the political cannot deal with this topic, but its treatment should be derived as a logical consequence of this introduction.

The type, the number and the names of the actors that in each historical circumstance occupy the position of monopoliser of compliance production is of no concern in this perspective. They could be chiefs, patriarchs, military commanders, elected officials, clerics, lords, leaders or prophets. What matters is the presence or absence in a given social field of an actor (individual or composite) who is recognised as having the de facto capacity to generate

---

24. In line with de Jouvenel's *law of conservative exclusion* discussed in chapter 2.

the compliance of the other actors in the field with her own final decisions. As I did with the confinement of actors, I will avoid going into the varieties of historical or geographical circumstances of monopolisation but instead focus on the ideal-typical aspects of manifestations of it. From this point of view, three linked and general features characterise the monopolisation of the production of behavioural compliance: an 'accumulation of enforcement resources', 'limitations' and 'depersonalisation and formalisation'.

Accumulation of enforcement resources

In a situation of monopolisation of compliance provision, a distinction exists between the provider of such compliance (the ruler) and those who have to comply with it (the ruled or the subjects). The monopolisation depends primarily on the effective capacity of the ruler to enforce compliance by the ruled. Even if the ruler can avail herself of persuasion, conditioning and manipulation, compliance eventually results from a credible threat to enforce. There is a general tendency, therefore, for the ruler to accumulate resources that guarantee the enforcement of his compliance requests. This is by far the most important feature of the monopolisation process.

From the theoretical point of view, we know little about this accumulation of enforcement resources by a third party. In a world of cheap and fully available information, both rulers and subjects can easily calculate the costs of resisting or yielding, tolerating or repressing. Enforcement resources need not be deployed, as the correct calculation will induce the losing side to acquiesce. However, information is neither cheap nor complete, uncertainties as to the costs of toleration and repression in any given circumstance exist, and therefore a considerable amount of uncertainty persists as to the capacity of the enforcer to effectively enforce the preferred outcomes. New alliances and a disintegration of previous alliances may occur, radically changing the balances and the perceptions of actors (recollections of resources in critical decision situations). Alliances and collective action mobilisation can involve external players; that is, other rulers, other military allies and so on. Subjects can mobilise new resources, inventing new mechanisms of collective action that reduce the costs they expect of resisting the enforcer. While the normal routine of associative life runs smoothly under the monopoliser's scrutiny, which usually finds some natural barrier to its unruly deployment (see the following section 'limitation'), cumbersome costly calculations and choices surround crucial issues. 'Absolute' enforcement is most costly, and a level of total unchallenged compliance is not only difficult to achieve but it is also uneconomical. It may also be unnecessary. Hence, the idea of an optimal level of enforcement resources.

In a rationalistic perspective, we can argue that the first problem for a ruler is to maintain his rulership and to accumulate enough resources to this end. The strength of this inclination is in direct proportion to the losses that the ruler would sustain in the case of termination of his role as enforcer. In membership fields, the ruler may depend too much on the consent of the ruled to risk his person, resources, relatives and connections in the rulership relations. In contrast, in territorial entities the ruler may face such huge costs if he loses the monopolistic position that he may be inclined to accumulate whatever resources he deems necessary to feel secure. In Renaissance principalities, much was at stake: wealth for sure and occasionally also life. In modern legalised and professionalised politics, politicians put only their positions at stake, and perhaps some limited material rewards, but not much more. In general, the more highly specified the rules for accessing, maintaining or losing the position of a monopolistic provider, the less is likely to be at stake for the ruler's person or family.

There is little theoretical literature on the problem of the accumulation of enforcement resources. The most interesting insights on this come from the 'new institutional economics' (NIE) literature on contract enforcement. This literature deals directly with the general problem of enforcement, which is usually under-conceptualised in other approaches, and it is therefore worth thoroughly analysing. Therefore, we should start with this solid body of knowledge. However, the assumptions that lie behind this approach generate some inconsistencies in the passage from private to public enforcement and considerably limit its applicability to the latter problem. We shall first review its contribution and subsequently point to its weak links.

The NIE literature sees enforcement as a general problem for every agreement among parties, both those which are self-enforced and those which are enforced by a third party.[25] 'What the enforcer enforces are "market" transactions, governed by contracts'.[26] At the onset of interactions, contracts have to be self-enforcing 'since no external organisation yet exists to offer third party enforcement'. However, at some later stage contracts can also be enforced by a 'private' third party – which is typically a dispute settlement mechanism (private courts, mediators, referees) – or enforced by a 'public authority' – typically courts (in private law) or administrative courts (in public law). Briefly, enforcement is the genus of which self-enforcement, private third-party

---

25. I take as a reference here the articles in Ménard, C. (ed.) (2000), *Institutions, Contracts and Organizations. Perspectives from New Institutional Economics*, Cheltenham, UK: Edward Elgar, and in particular Barzel, Yoram, *The State and the Diversity of Third-Party Enforcers*, pp. 211–33; and Mantzavinos, C. (2001), *Individuals, Institutions and Markets*, Cambridge: Cambridge University Press.

26. Barzel, Yoram (2000), *The State and the Diversity of Third-Party Enforcers*, p. 218.

enforcement and public third-party enforcement are species. The reference point for ascertaining optimal enforcement resources is always the costs and advantages of different types of enforcement for the enforced parties.

There are specific advantages of contracts enforced by third parties. Agreements are relations that individuals are free to form or not, and individuals who perceive the potential for a profitable agreement among them will ask a third party to enforce it if they expect to gain from the enforcement. At a cost, third parties provide the contracting parties 'with an altered set of incentives such that they expect their net gains from interacting to exceed what they could obtain under self-enforcement'. 'In their relationship with one another, then, third parties and their clients, whether individually or collectively, must perceive that the gain from maintaining their relations in the future will exceed whatever gains they may reap from reneging on their agreement in the present'.[27] In other words, in this literature the third-party enforcer appears as (a) agreed by the enforced parties; (b) functionally facilitating; and (c) specialised in the transaction, that is, with no ambitions of his own to use enforcement resources for other aims. Third parties offer 'services', and these are subject to forces of supply and demand.

Parties particularly benefit from third-party enforcement when they perceive that the value of the venture may become negative in the future (e.g., in the case of loans, without third-party enforcement the borrower will immediately renege). Similarly, they benefit when the third party may offer the parties deals that generate greater joint advantages than they could generate on their own. 'The parties would gain from the assistance of a third party in ensuring that the ventures will be undertaken and continued as long as their *joint* value remains positive'.[28] Note that in every instant the parties remain the judges who decide whether the services of the third party, and thus the costs, are worth the gain from the enhanced interaction. The value of third-party enforcement is always measured from their point of view.

So far so good, as far as private third-party enforcement of agreements is concerned. One should note, however, that a vicious circle emerges at the level of self-enforced agreements or private third-party–enforced agreements. For a transaction to take place, it is necessary first to define the rights over what is exchanged. It is not clear who enforces (and therefore protects) these property rights on which self-enforced or private third-party–enforced contracts depend. Property rights themselves seem in need of enforcement (and of an enforcer) so as not to be violated or challenged, as evidence suggests that acquisition, maintenance and transmission of them have been quite contentious issues in human history. Nevertheless, *postulating* the safe existence

---

27. Ibid., pp. 217, 211 and 212, respectively.
28. Ibid., p. 213.

of property rights the costs/advantages of a private third party monopolistically providing compliance can be convincingly analysed.

On these premises, this literature slides from enforcement of agreements by a private enforcer towards the special case of a 'public' enforcer. A public enforcer is a special type of enforcer, defined by its capacity to inflict harm. 'Where there are not enduring direct relationships between them and the enforced individuals, the enforcers impose costs by inflicting harm. The latter enforcement form is the heart of the state'.[29] The difference between private and public enforcers rests on the 'length' of the relationship between the enforcer and the enforced, which generates momentous consequences. Unlike enforcement based on long-term relations between the enforcer and the enforced, when the enforcer is not bound to his 'clients' by a long-term relationship the use of violence and coercion emerges as a possibility. In other words, the presence of an enforcer who is not chosen by the parties and who is not bound to entertain a long-term relationship with them changes the situation because he can use violence, imposing direct costs in the form of confiscation of the gains his enforcement generates. This therefore becomes extremely dangerous for the enforced. The ruler monopolises the granting of licenses for private activities. The ruler can directly monopolise an entire business process. Monopolies are an easy way to raise tax that may be more effective than taxing the surpluses of private economic agents. In both cases, she extracts a rent from these activities.

Obviously, parties will not seek the support of a 'public' third party if they expect her to confiscate their gains. 'A dictator who does not commit not to confiscate is deprived, then, of the potential income that third-party enforcement services may generate' because they would refuse to use his service. However, the enforced cannot avoid this risk ex post. Their only possibility is to avoid it ex ante, via cooperation through a collective action mechanism capable of controlling the third (public) party. In doing this they can try to commit the third party to not confiscating.[30] The collective action mechanism should generate a power that equals or exceeds the power of violence by the third-party enforcer, or at least would be sufficient to force the third party to accurately calculate the costs of repression or toleration of the collective action mechanism.

Summing up, therefore, the enforcer induces the parties to an agreement to perform when they would not have performed on their own by threatening to impose costs on them. However, when the subjects 'realise that the enforcer engages in extortion, they will reduce the use of his services and may discontinue using them altogether'. They may join a different third party – *which*

---

29. Ibid., p. 211.
30. Ibid., pp. 216–17.

assumes that there is no monopoly of compliance production – or they may exit the relationship – *which assumes that the actors are not confined*.

In this passage from private to public enforcers, it is no longer clear who the public enforcer is that faces competitive alternatives and from whom exit is possible. An enforcer who acts on request and who is idle if nobody wants him to act cannot be the 'state' or any monopolistic provider of behavioural compliance as I have defined. An enforcer who acts using violence and confiscation is not likely to be discarded as an enforcer, and in principle he can confiscate the entire property. Obviously, this second one could be the 'state'. In other words, this approach must take as a reference a field in which there is a monopolistic enforcer, but actors are free to use its enforcement services or not; that is, they are free to exit and are therefore non-confined in the relationship. In chapter 4 I will discuss this specific type of field at length. The conclusion so far is that, if we want to avoid entering a second vicious circle, this conceptualisation is valid only for one type of field – the open fields – but not for all.

One may argue that increasing the level of resources will tend to make the level of resistance fall, so that the ruler will have to spend fewer resources and will have to fully deploy them more rarely. Similarly, if the constituency of a monopolistic enforcer increases (by dynastic accretion, conquest or marriage), the number of actors over which he can exercise his powers increases correspondingly, and the enlarged constituency may induce the enforcer to increase his enforcement resources. However, monopolistic providers of compliance cannot simply use systematic violence. They must consider whether their present actions as enforcers using violence may affect subsequent ones. Inflicting punishment is costly.

To resist enforcement by collective action is also costly. However, to the extent that they can act collectively, the subjects of an extended constituency in principle need fewer resources to contain the enforcer than would be necessary for a smaller group. Below a certain level, there are too few actors to contrast even a slight asymmetry of resources. Up to a certain group size, the decrease in the costs of resistance via collective action is greater than the increase in the power of enforcement resulting from the increased size of the group. Above a certain group size, enforcement needs may prompt a conspicuous growth in the enforcement resources of the ruler. In medium-sized communities, a balance exists in which an increase in the powers of the enforcer to face the complex problems and requests of the community is less than the reduction in the resistance costs to the subjects due to their number. This is the key to understanding the rather egalitarian and power-sharing nature of small-sized communities.[31] Note also that a medium-sized community can

---

31. Ibid., pp. 220–21.

abate the problems of collective action more easily, or prevent them from arising to begin with. Collective action mechanisms do not need to produce a collective good. They may reduce the risks and costs of repression to those associated with the mechanisms and may not do so for the others, thereby inducing participation on a selective incentive basis.

We have stayed with the insights from the new institutional economics literature for a while, because they directly tackle the general problem of enforcement, which is usually under-conceptualised in other approaches. At the same time, I have pointed out a few inconsistencies that derive from an uncritical transposition of the problem of contract enforcement among contracting partners to the enforcement of non-contracts among a ruler and subjects. Both when and how we move from an agreed and accepted third-party enforcer of private agreements (whose property rights remain, however, without an enforcer) to a public monopolistic enforcer from which there is no exit and whose enforcement resources may extend far beyond any agreed remit remains mysterious and obscure.

In my view, the inconsistencies generated by this line of thought depend on the view of the ruler-ruled relationship being exclusively centred on the enforcement of private deals, on the one hand, and on the confiscation of gains by the ruler, on the other hand. The excessive focus on this single dimension of ruler/ruled exchanges perhaps hides the mechanism for the accumulation of enforcement resources by the monopolistic provider of compliance. The ruler and the ruled are exclusively viewed in the light of their respective capacities to confiscate and to resist confiscation by collective action mechanisms. This creates a similitude to the private enforcer whose services can be refused. However, this approach – and in general any theory of predatory rulership that focuses exclusively on predatory inclinations of rulers and revenue-maximisation goals[32] – overlooks the fact that a monopolistic enforcer accumulates and has at his disposal resources to generate behavioural compliance *in several connected areas* and *on issues not confined to property rights*. Similarly and consequently, subjects control resources essential to the ruler in seemingly diverse and connected areas. The result is that the exchanges that take place between rulers and the ruled are considerably more complex and multifaceted. What the ruler needs to achieve through compliance and offers of compensation for it and what the subjects achieve through compliance and offers in exchange are far more complex than a deal on the confiscation/non-confiscation of property.

---

32. Such as Levi, M. (1988), *On Rule and Revenue*, Berkeley: University of California Press; Charap, Joshua and Christian Harm (2000), 'Institutionalized Corruption and the Kleptocratic State', in C. Ménard (ed.), *Institutions, Contracts and Organizations*, pp. 188–208; and Barzel, Y. (2002), *A Theory of the State: Economic Rights, Legal Rights, and the Scope of the State*, Cambridge: Cambridge University Press.

First, as I have hinted before, the ruler offers a good that neither private self-enforcing nor private third-party–enforced agreements can provide. This is the guarantee that agreements freely reached among the parties (with or without the facilitating role of a third-party private enforcer) are valid for the entire community of the ruled, including individuals who are external to the agreements. Put differently, the ruler extends and guarantees to the entire field the validity of those rights on which private dealings depend. In even simpler terms, the ruler guarantees property rights not to the parties but to the membership of the entire field. Framed in a different form again, the ruler reduces the numbers of gangs and bandits in the environment that aim at *individual* predation. The approach emphasising agreements by private parties on established property rights ipso facto excludes this factor by assuming the safe existence of property rights. Although the difficulty of enforcing private agreements is thoroughly analysed in this approach, in assuming that private deals are valid for and accepted by the entire field – and that they constitute the basis of the subjects' capacity to resist the ruler – the theory presupposes the existence of what it is trying to constitute: the monopolistic provider. The theoretical argument bounces backwards and forwards between private and public enforcers as in a three-card trick in which at any particular time one is uncertain about the whereabouts of the true underpinning authority.

The possibility that the third actor specialised in the production of behavioural conformity abuses this capacity is intrinsic to his position and is a danger embedded in the very constitution of this kind of actor. However, we should not overlook the fact that expropriation or 'rents' levied by rulers are the other inseparable face of their main responsibility for the constitution and defence of those same guaranteed rights (to property, life, etc.) on which the benevolent view of private dealings and contracts rests.[33]

Moreover, enforcement by the third public party concerns not only private property rights but also competencies, faculties, titles and so on which are guaranteed not only among parties but also between enforcers and parties (licenses, monopolies, granted powers, administrative authorisations, levies, taxes, military duties, etc.). In a sense, although public authorities may help to enforce 'contracts', they primarily enforce things that are not contracts (not synallagmatic) but are rather guaranteed rights or powers that qualify the further claims of parties.

---

33. Abuse based on the self-interest of the ruler and rent-seeking activities by those possessing political power has often been regarded not only as dangerous for subjects but also as affecting overall social efficiency and economic performance through history. See North, Douglass (1981), *Structure and Change in Economic History*, New York: W.W. Norton; North, Douglass and Barry Weingast (1989), 'Constitutions and Commitments: The Evolution of Institutions Governing Public Choice in 17th Century England', *Journal of Economic History*, 49: 803–32. The critique in the text applies particularly well to this literature.

The point is that too much emphasis on the dyadic relationship between ruler and ruled in terms of rent extraction and exploitation of the latter by the former overlooks the extent to which a monopolisation of rule is constitutive of those same guaranteed rights – often results of private predation – on which the concepts of predation and rent extraction are based.[34] This is tantamount to saying that 'political inefficiencies' ground the 'economic efficiencies' against which they are measured. Along these lines, Gary Miller and Thomas Hammond argue that political limitations to economic efficiency are unavoidable and are not a historical contingency but a logical inevitability.[35] My argument is different. It underlines that without 'political inefficiencies' the property rights with which economic efficiency is evaluated would not exist or would be highly unstable. Consequently, the calculus of economic efficiency is built on the political inefficiency of the foundation of property rights and is then used to measure this inefficiency.

There is here a devaluation of evidence that the presence of a third-actor monopoliser of compliance production may prevent or attenuate other kinds of expropriation and rent-seeking emerging from the social relationship in more anarchic situations. Although in general one may recognise the specific position of the ruler and its capacity to generate compliance as being particularly dangerous, one should not regard this as the only form of 'economic inefficiency'. In other words, there is no reason to believe that, in fields without a monopolistic enforcer or with a weak one, expropriation and predation are excluded and therefore are unproblematic. There might be room, therefore, to improve the 'efficiency' of institutions to reduce the ruler's capacity to expropriate. However, we must also recognise that centralisation and monopolisation of compliance production is accompanied by a constitution of individual- and group-guaranteed rights and by a decrease in other, more private and previously poorly sanctioned predatory activities.

An exclusive focus on predation by the ruler and resistance to predation by the ruled makes it more difficult to understand the phenomena of monopolisation and accumulation of enforcement resources. It is extremely problematic to explain why individuals, who are assumed to hold rights and property, should take the enormous risk of accepting the monopolisation of compliance production. It becomes much easier to understand this passage if we recognise that these same rights, based on which one hypothesises a difficulty in constituting a monopolistic ruler, were first constituted, generalised

---

34. This, *mutatis mutandis*, is a reformulation of the well-known position of Thomas Hobbes on the relationship between property rights and the ruler elaborated in *De Cive*, Ch. 19, and *Leviathan*, Ch. 29.

35. Miller, Gary and Thomas Hammond (1994), 'Why Politics Is More Fundamental Than Economics. Incentive-Compatible Mechanisms Are Not Credible', *Journal of Theoretical Politics*, 6: 5–26, p. 8.

and stabilised by the ruler's production of compliance. This is what lowers the cost to any private party of constantly defending her specific acquisition of values. The ruler extracts rents that he himself had basically constituted for individuals and groups. Under these conditions, the ruled/ruler 'exchange' becomes much more comprehensible.

Moreover, in addition to this constitutive generation of subjective rights, the successive enforcement of agreements based on them and the adjudication of torts among parties at their request, the ruler was also responsible for many other primordial 'public goods' – what mediaeval thinking called *imperium*, as opposed to *jurisdictio*. *Jurisdictio* is the power to decide on controversies among subjects establishing the rights and duties of parties based on written or consuetudinary law. *Gubernaculum*, or *imperium*, is the power to manage those issues and affairs that individual subjects cannot manage, such as external relations, internal security and general interest activities. Decisions by the *imperium* represented unilateral engagements by the ruler mainly concerning the way in which his powers would be exercised and the people or functionaries to which that function was delegated (like the police, for instance). In a sense, the *gubernaculum* was a material power without juridical effects.

To sum up this argument, the 'calculus' of the ruler and the ruled is not and never was as simple as in private contract enforcement concerning property, and exchanges between the ruled and rulers cannot be reduced to property predation and confiscation. In the connection between the ruler and the ruled, the calculations must have been multidimensional and very difficult on both sides. Rulership has differentiated functionally since the beginning, and it has always included complex functions with respect to which a simple calculus of expropriation of property and defence of property is oversimplified. This latter view maximises the similitude between contracts among private parties and ruler/ruled exchanges at the cost of a trivial neo-contractualist assimilation of politics to law or economics.

Limitations

The ruler/subject relationship and the optimal level of accumulation of enforcement resources are analysed in a more realistic fashion and are far more comprehensible if we explicitly consider their multifaceted nature, as mentioned earlier. This highlights the inherent powerful *limitations* on rulers' appetites embedded in the crucial resources held by subjects. Limitations on the endless accumulation of enforcement resources and on predatory impulses are built into the process of monopolisation itself when one takes into consideration its multifaceted character. Brunner offers a superb elucidation of the process of command monopolisation leading to the modern concept of 'sovereignty' – the monopolisation we know best: the passage from the mediaeval system to the modern state in Europe.[36] He highlights that the essence of a landlord's power is constituted by the plurality of functions included in it: *Schutz*, the concept of defence in war; *Schirm*, the concept of justice; *Rat*, the concept of counsel in the Diet; and *Hilfe*, the concept of taxation in war and in peace. The mutual obligations resulting from these, whether they are towards superiors, offering *Schutz* and *Schirm* (defence and justice), or inferiors, offering *Rat* and *Hilfe* (advice and support), also correspond to the goals of the community. The mutual obligations of *Schirm* and *Rat* (justice and advice) were crucial for internal peace. Those of *Schutz* and *Hilfe* (defence and support) were crucial in the search for external peace or to follow ambitions. They all operate across the concrete network of *Herrschaft* (lordships), of the various kinds that constituted the 'constitutional' structure of mediaeval political formations.

Internal peace monopolisation required overcoming the many forms of self-defence rights, such as the prominent right to 'feud', which was hard to eradicate. 'If in the territorial court the landlord appears only in his capacity of presiding judge, in the case of *defensio* (defence), on the contrary, he presents himself in his capacity as head of the territorial community, with power to command and discipline'.[37] In other words, the authority of the ruler had other dimensions beyond the functions of justice (contract enforcement and tort redemption) and support (resource extraction). It included the function of internal peace, which presupposed the elimination of other internal sources of compliance or private justices in the form of the 'feud'. It included the form of *Rat*, which implied consultation with and taking advice from other relevant actors. It also included the crucial dimensions of defence and war, which must have radically altered any calculation based on contract enforcement and the risks of expropriation.

Extension of the area of command and the relative accumulation of enforcement resources can also be highly contested by relevant political actors, as it was in the passage from the Middle Ages to absolutist modern states. Nobles, local lords, church authorities, cities with privileges, knights and their troops, all at times objected to and opposed the monopolisation of rule. As there are many complex ways in which an instigation transforms into a command, so there are many ways to oppose and challenge it. Although we may hypothesise that truly competing instigations capable of jeopardising the existence of the group are deactivated to begin with by filtering, channelling and manipulating, an expansion of command to new issues and

---

36. Brunner, Otto (1898; 1984), *Land und Herrschaft: Grundfragen der territorialen Verfassungsgeschichte Österreichs im Mittelalter*, Darmstadt: Wissenschaftliche Buchgesellschaft.
37. Ibid., p. 360, my translation. On Territorial Lords (*Landesherrschaft*), see in particular chapter 5, pp. 357–440.

domains is always open to contestation. Opponents can challenge the procedure with which a specific command has been selected without nonetheless denying that command must be achieved. More interestingly, opponents may argue that an instigation selected to become a command is one for which a diversity of competing instigations could be tolerated. They can claim that different instigations are incompatible at the level of each single individual but compatible at the level of the group, arguing, therefore, that the diverse instigations could be left with their status of competing – not conflicting – instigations, everyone being free to adhere to one, another or none without any need for a command to exclude some of them (typical examples are various cultural stigmata, such as religions, languages and ethnicities). Note that this second challenge denies the necessity of a command selection on a given issue. Any polity in any historical moment, including the contemporary, has to face the problem of the frontier between the area of command and that of free competing instigations. Note that in discussing the more or less polyarchic nature of contemporary polities we refer to all these contestation mechanisms: the way in which a command is arrived at among a set of instigations; the extent to which an issue is regarded as conflicting as opposed to competitive; *and also* the extent to which an issue on which a command has been proclaimed may be continually raised again on account of contestation over the first two points.

The environment of the ruler also includes competition with alternative external rulers. Rulers may be more sensitive to the need to secure their holdings vis-à-vis external competitors than vis-à-vis internal claimants. The accumulation of enforcement resources may be driven by the need to stabilise control of the territory against potential external intruders, and the ruler may have an interest in expanding the territory and the people under his control, as well as in creating 'loyalties' among the subjects that enhance his capacities.[38] On the one hand, external threats are likely to make accumulation of enforcement resources by the ruler easier.[39] On the other hand, under

---

38. See Tilly, C. (1990), *Coercion, Capital, and European States, A.D. 990–1992*, Cambridge: Blackwell, especially pp. 67–96 on the role of war in state-making.

39. Several thinkers have highlighted the link between external threats and internal justice (contract enforcement). Erasmus commented, 'I am loth to suspect here what only too often, alas!, has turned to be the truth: that the rumour of war with the Turks has been trumped up with the purpose of mulcting the Christian Population, so that being burned and crushed in all possible ways it might be all the more servile towards the tyranny of both kinds of princes (ecclesiastical and secular)'. Erasmus of Rotterdam (1536; 1964), *The 'Adages' of Erasmus*, edited and translated by M. Mann Phillips, Cambridge: Cambridge University Press, pp. 347–48. Rousseau reminded us that 'war and conquest without and the encroachment of despotism within give each other mutual support. . . . Aggressive princes wage war at least as much on their subjects as on their enemies and the conquering nation is left no better off than the conquered'. Rousseau, J.J. (1756), 'Judgement of Saint Pierre's Project for Perpetual Peace', in S. Hoffman and D.P. Fidler (eds.) (1981), *Rousseau on International Relations*, Oxford: Clarendon Press, p. 91.

an external threat a powerful force unites subjects and rulers, which is existentially prior to any problem of internal resistance against the enforcer. This is the fear of alternative rulers and alternative peoples who could invade and occupy, expropriate or even exterminate. In fact, it is likely that the risks of exploitation and confiscation come more frequently from external invasion and conquest than from internal abuse.

The English Glorious Revolution has been interpreted as the paradigmatic case of the capacity of subjects (the relevant ones) to force the ruler into a credible commitment to not expropriate.[40] Even if one omits the many other dimensions of the interregnum conflicts that contributed to shaping the outcome – the Catholic/Protestant dynastic issue, the social challenges posed by the Levellers, the Diggers and other similar movements, the messianism of the Fifth Monarchists and many other radical sects – this interpretation undervalues the confining conditions of its validity. This was perhaps a rather exceptional, if not unique, case in which the easily defendable territorial circumscription (an unconquerable island kingdom) made external threats very feeble. In cases in which, as with England, a true external threat is minimal or null, confrontation between the ruler and the relevant ruled actors more easily takes the form of collective action mechanisms to check the ruler's ambitions. This point concerns the crucial connection between defence of the external boundary and internal political structuring. Insightful minds of the time underlined this, as is evidenced in the quotations in footnote 39 from Erasmus and Rousseau, as did later historical scholarship. In a famous quote, Robert Seeley stated that 'the degree of political freedom within a state must reasonably be inversely proportional to the military and political pressures on its borders'.[41] Hintze alludes to this relationship when he argues that 'notwithstanding its heavy commitment in continental war, bureaucratic centralism did not develop in Britain because its isolation meant that it did not have to raise and administer a large standing army. Its strength rested upon the navy and navies do not shape the apparatus of government as do armies'.[42] Finer suggests that one cannot understand why French historians are so obsessed with the 'demon' of exit while the British are equally interested in the 'angel' of voice, without taking into account the fact that France's borders were disputed up to World War II, whereas Britain's borders are more or less the same today as they were in 975.[43] These favourable territorial conditions fostered

---

40. North and Weingast, 'Constitutions and Commitments: The Evolution of Institutions Governing Public Choice in 17th Century England'.
41. Quoted in Hintze, O. (1962), *Staat und Verfassung*, edited by G. Oestreich, Göttingen: Vandenhoeck and Ruprecht, p. 366.
42. Hintze, *Staat und Verfassung*, pp. 415 and 428.
43. Finer, S.E. (1974), 'State-Building, State Boundaries and Border Control: An Essay on Certain Aspects of the First Phase of State-Building in Western Europe Considered in the Light of the Rokkan-Hirschman Model', *Social Science Information* 13: 79–126, esp. p. 115.

an explosion of internal voice in England in the first half of the seventeenth century. Interestingly enough, in the turmoil of the time the privileged direct observer Thomas Hobbes was more obsessed with the risk of private predation – which he labelled 'neighbour predation' – than with the risk of state predation.

The combination of domestic (within-field) exchanges and external (extra-field) menaces is probably the key to the drive for a continual accumulation of enforcement powers by rulers. Much as external threats and shocks work to increase the coercion power of enforcers beyond what subjects are normally willing to accept, they can also work to reduce exploitation and to strengthen the links between rulers and subjects, whose support against the pretensions and threats of external rulers is essential. The conclusion is that the process of monopolisation results from an accumulation of previously structurally differentiated competences and resources slowly brought to bear on the person of the ruler. Combining the mediaeval functionally separated activities of *Schutz*, *Schirm*, *Rat*, and *Hilfe* must have been a rather complex process in the monopolisation of command that led to absolutist solutions. The 'calculations' of rulers and ruled on this multidimensional functional space were unlikely to yield clear-cut equilibria, even before religious splits and wars further complicated the calculus. Any focus on a single dimension, such as predation, is likely to miss the essence of the process and of its acceptance.

Therefore, a monopolisation of compliance production in whatever field is hardly unconstrained and unlimited, as it rests on a combination of the aforementioned functions and relationships. Even the radical reconstruction of the origins of modern absolutism in Carl Schmitt's theory of dictatorship continually mentions the innumerable juridical and factual limitations to absolutist rule.[44] Since the beginning, any monopolisation has had to take into account 'both its own dependence and its own impact on some non-political resources and practices'.[45] The monopolistic provider must recognise the existence of other fields of interaction in which the group members are involved and which should be excluded from interference to avoid jeopardising the command achieved in the field of its own concern.[46] For instance, the ruler faces limits to his capacity to command in areas that are preserved from

---

44. Schmitt, Carl (1921), *Dictatorship*, Cambridge: Polity Press, 2013, pp. 1–179 (*Die Diktatur*, Berlin: Dunker &, Humblot).

45. Poggi, G. (1990), *The State: Its Nature, Development, and Prospects*, London: Polity Press, pp. 35–42.

46. Popitz (1992), *Phaenomene der Macht* deals with this dimension, defining it as 'integration'. However, his treatment is closely associated with the institutionalisation of power within the state, and it is ill-suited to my purpose here. It mainly refers to what can be called the 'autonomy of subsystems' within a political system.

interference by customs, traditions, social norms, religious and spiritual concerns and so on. The ruler can accept that in pursuit of their economic affairs or of their spiritual concerns individuals can bind themselves with agreements and associations – that is, they can build other 'authorities' – but he will nevertheless claim that the 'bindingness' of these will in the end depend on his at least implicit acceptance. The ruler may recognise and guarantee such relationships only as long as they do not endanger the monopolisation of compliance production itself. In fact, when manifestations of these private dealings generate identifiable interests and demands for voice, organisation or association, the ruler can present himself as the defender of the unity of the community against such divisions and conflicts. A considerable amount of planning and justification discourses concerning public interest, states of necessity, exceptional circumstances and other rationales of various natures usually accompany these arguments, among which legal discourses are particularly important.

Finally, we should not forget that the process of monopolisation of command does not need to be of the territorial type referred in the previous examples. It does occur also in functionally defined fields. Monopolisation of command exists within all forms of organisational and associational life, without resting on the confinement of actors that is typical of the territorial units. In these cases, a complex relationship must develop between the monopolistic provider in any given field and the monopolistic provider of other fields. As mentioned, this was the typical situation of the Middle Ages pluralism. The same situation occurs in modern polities characterised by a multiplicity of fields with a monopolistic provider whose production of compliance is limited in a functional way to a predefined number of subjects that are not confined. Abuse of command is less of a problem in these open fields, where it will meet with a declining membership or a collapse of the group, given that in this case the members can exit the social relationship. The new institutional economics description of enforcement discussed earlier applies more correctly to these situations. In these cases, subjects rightly correspond to 'customers' who calculate the advantages of the monopolisation function against its costs. Eventually, if they are dissatisfied, they can select a different third-party enforcer and switch to using its services. In short, what the NIE literature says about the enforcer-enforced relationship properly applies to non-confinement situations of actors.

Although there are limits built into abuses in the production of compliance, abuse remains a possibility in any circumstance of monopolisation of command, particularly under special and exceptional circumstances in which the factuality of problem solving imposes itself on the normativity of the relationships in the field.

Depersonalisation and formalisation

A general tendency associated with the process of monopolisation is for commands to be issued by people who act in a capacity of occupants of *roles* and no longer as specific individual issuers of orders and commands. These roles may become highly differentiated by level, by organs, by faculties and facilities of rule. Most of these differentiations tend to take a juridical texture, such as the hierarchy of norms, the layering of the judicial system, phases of administrative implementation, selection of political and administrative personnel and so on.[47]

In the process of monopolisation, requests for behavioural compliance also tend to formalise. To be valid, orders need to be expressed in certain ways, to respect certain procedures. They cannot simply be *fiats* devoid of such correct ways of expression. Progressively, therefore, even in the most traditional systems of social relationships the nature of command is contingent on and constrained by the form of its expression, both in its legitimacy and effectiveness dimensions. These establish where, when and by means of which procedures commands can be deliberated and, again, in which forms they have to be communicated. In its most developed forms, this formalisation is characterised by a predominance of legal language and legal reasoning. Compliance requests in the form of commands are formalised through the use of specific language which is eventually the juridical discourse derived from or inspired by long-standing and long-appreciated legal traditions, such as Roman law, canonical law or common law. This legal discourse has certain characteristics: it is text-based discourse; it traditionally has a strong conceptual content; it also shows a constitutive orientation to abstraction and systematisation (although this differs in different legal traditions).[48]

Because of these features, such legal discourse is able to generate sophisticated reasoning, a capacity to subsume specific circumstances under general principles, or to relate specific cases to previously decided 'similar' cases, and arrive at conclusions through syllogistic arguments. Using these techniques, legal reasoning arrives at selecting one answer from within a set of possible ones. The formal quality of the reasoning that leads to the answer – logical rigor, consistency, reference to doctrine and recognised authority,

---

47. For the categories of 'personalisation' and 'formalisation', I draw on the treatment in Popitz (1992), *Phaenomene der Macht*, pp. 233–60 and the discussion in Poggi, *Varieties of Political Experiences*, chapter 5, pp. 53–62. I try here to disentangle these categories from their primary reference to the state.

48. There are relatively rare cases in which this trend is not observable or is reverted. They are limited to special post-colonial situations, which Linz and Chehabi conceptualise as 'sultanistic regimes'. See Chebabi, Houchang E. and Juan J. Linz (eds.) (1998), *Sultanistic Regimes*, Baltimore: Johns Hopkins University Press, pp. 3–25.

compatibility with other sources of norms – is its primary evaluation criteria. For all these reasons, in the West for centuries legal training and legal language constituted the most sophisticated and rewarding source of discourse, attracted bright young intellectuals, had enormous social prestige and staffed the operational branches of the modern state.[49]

---

49. The entire book by Poggi devoted to the state gives special attention and importance to the parallel development of monopolisation, legal techniques and the professionalisation of the legal profession. Poggi, *The State: Its Nature, Development, and Prospects*.

Chapter 4

Fields of political action

TYPES OF FIELDS

Following the discussion in chapter 3, every field of social relationships can be defined as 'open' or 'closed' depending on the level of confinement of the actors involved, and as 'monopolised' or 'non-monopolised' depending on the presence or absence of a third actor specialised in the production of behavioural compliance for the entire field. Closedness forces the emergence of 'political' interactions based on the need to obtain the compliance of other subjects in view of achieving one's own goal. Monopolisation suspends the naturally scattered search for compliance among a plurality of actors, each aiming at a necessary quota of conformity from the others. These two dimensions are the constitutive categories of the most significant political experience. Combining the two dimensions yields the four types of fields illustrated in figure 4.1.

I label fields that are both open and devoid of a monopolisation of command *anarchic fields*. I label fields and related social relationships that are open but present an actor specialised in the production of compliance *authority fields*. In the column for closed fields, the monopolisation dimension operates the distinction between *natural fields* and *governmental fields*.[1] In the former, actors are confined but no monopolisation of command is available. In the latter, the presence of an actor with the specific task of compliance

---

1. As mentioned in a previous footnote, Lasswell first introduced the concept of 'governmental arena'. The inspiration for the distinction between natural and governmental arenas comes from Stoppino, Mario (2001), *Potere e teoria politica*, Milano: Giuffré. Stoppino's terminology is slightly different, however. Other authors use the expressions 'authority' or 'monetary' arena for what is here labelled a 'governmental field'. My terminological preference is simply due to my intention to maintain conceptual consistency throughout this book.

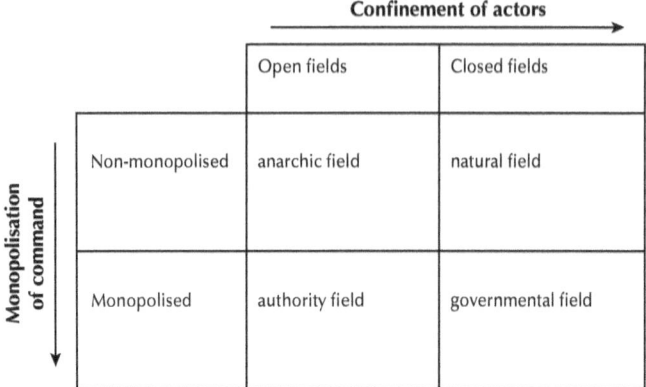

Figure 4.1. Types of interaction fields

production couples with confinement of the actors'. The typology is simple enough. I hope to show that its implications for the analysis of the political clarify things in several respects.

Anarchic fields

With no confinement and no actor specialised in the production of compliance, political action is hardly a relevant category in this field. The essential characteristic of political relationships – compliance – is either not present or very tenuous. There can be no attempt to achieve compliance. Whatever the basis of the relationship among actors, from intimacy to affection, from economic exchange to cooperation towards common goals, what happens in the field can only be the result of consensus, emotional solidarity, negotiated agreements or synallagmatic exchanges among subsets of actors. Any form of cooperation and collective action is merely voluntary, with the purpose of achieving joint goals that are otherwise not available. The absence of any possibility of achieving undesired compliance against one's will gives these collective actions limited relevance from the political point of view.

The work of persuasion, manipulation and, possibly, some level of environmental conditioning can generate compliance primarily based on reference to loyalty, identity, affection and so on. Sanctioning is by definition impossible. Even the long chain of environmental conditioning of other actors is very difficult indeed. When resources cannot affect other non-confined actors, the field depends on voluntary relations.[2] I leave it to the reader to identify relationships characterised by these features. As an indication, we can mention all peer

---

2. A point underlined in Warren, M.E. (1999), 'What Is Political?', *Journal of Theoretical Politics*, 11: 207–31, p. 230.

groups, collective leisure activities, social exchanges of any sort and even the relationship between buyers and sellers in the ideal market. Actors in anarchic fields may easily become entrapped in non-cooperative games – in which, however, the possibility of not playing is guaranteed – and they may also fail to realise gains from cooperation that are in principle possible. In such a field, only moves aiming at the confinement of other actors can satisfy a desire for command. Therefore, the equilibria reached have a feeble political intensity and are of relatively minor interest from the political point of view.

Of course, the category of exchanges, or voluntary exchanges, is far more intricate than presented here. Each party enters an exchange for reasons that are independent of the motives of the other partner. The formal shell of a voluntary exchange may in fact hide asymmetries that profoundly affect its voluntariness. The idea of synallagmatic exchanges stresses mutual obligations and avoids some problems but does not solve them all. To the extent that these exchanges imply 'joint action', it is usually argued that they are only authentic if they are based on shared intentions, or else grounded on the autonomy of the agents involved. However, there are also joint actions by agents without them sharing a common intention.[3] I try to limit these complications by discussing the pure category of 'exchanges' and 'joint actions' under the ideal assumption of the partners having unlimited and uncostly exit options. Although this theoretical state may be hard to realise in practice (as it is likely that there are always some costs of exit and therefore some limitation to it), such a postulation avoids entering into more complex discussions of shared intentionality, of genuine autonomy of actors and of potential asymmetry among them. The latter are made immaterial by the total exit option. In a pure anarchic field, an actor with doubts and reservations about the true intentions of potential partners, his own autonomy or a possible asymmetry of resources would simply leave the social relationship and escape the interaction. If she is not able to do so, it means that the actor is in some way confined and compelled to interact, and this crucial change makes the anarchic field slide into another type, namely, into a natural field.

This last point allows me to specify that an anarchic field as defined here does not fit into the realm of 'anarchic' international relations identified in the realist or neo-realist state-centric literature.[4] International relations theory widely resorts to the idea of an anarchic field of interaction for states in a world system devoid of a universal sovereign or worldwide government or

---

3. For the complications that I do not discuss in detail here, see Julius, A.J. (2013), 'The Possibility of Exchange', *Politics, Philosophy & Economics*, 12: 361–74; and Bratman, Michael (2009), 'Intention, Practical Rationality, and Self-Governance', *Ethics*, 119: 411–43.

4. Morgenthau, Hans (1948; 1978, 5th ed.), *Politics among Nations: The Struggle for Power and Peace*, New York: Alfred A. Knopf; Waltz, Kenneth (1954), *Man, the State, and War: A Theoretical Analysis*, New York: Columbia University Press.

hierarchical superiors. In other words, it takes as a starting point the absence of the monopolisation of compliance production and of a third actor specialised in this function at the world level. However, the actors – that is, states – are confined and can hardly subtract themselves from undesired interactions when they find themselves in situations of accentuated asymmetry. This means that states are forced to enter competition, conflict, cooperation and negotiation interaction modes. In my understanding, the state of an anarchic field is characterised by both the absence of monopolisation *and* the absence of confinement. In my framework, therefore, realistic international relations are best described as a 'natural' field rather than an 'anarchic' one (see the section on natural fields).

Authority fields

In *authority fields*, actors are free to leave social relationships, although an actor exists in the field which is specialised in the production of rules and of conformity with them. The members recognise the authority as essential to the achievement of the goals for which the field was set up to begin with. These are fields of functional authority and enforcement. The constant availability of exit options works as a guarantee that the authority exercised will be limited to the functional domain for which the field emerged. At the same time, the sheer presence of an authority generates the possibility that it may act in such a way as to try to confine the actors in the field beyond its functional scope. With its production, the authority in the field may try to increase the costs of exit.[5] Authority fields avoid facing any constitutive predicaments because of the voluntary adhesion of their members, and the freedom to exit frees their internal order from highly constraining political elements.

This analytical configuration covers a large variety of concrete situations of interactions among actors under functional authority. In principle, public bureaucracies, business organisations (whether they are organised as sole proprietorships, partnerships, corporations or cooperatives) and true voluntary associations (societies, guilds, clubs, confraternities, unions, parties, leagues, sects, partnerships and fellowships) present this analytical configuration of interaction among their members. Several other features distinguish among these different types of authority fields. In line with the analytical preference of this book, I will not enter into a detailed investigation of these

---

5. Eckstein's previously discussed position is that politics is embedded in any kind of authority structure, also including, therefore, fields in which the actors are not confined. Eckstein, H. (1973), 'Authority Patterns: A Structural Basis for Political Enquiry', *American Political Science Review*, 63: 1114–1161. In my view, politics as political action characterises every field and not only authority and governmental fields. The difference lies in the type of behavioural compliance that can be achieved in the different fields, which is what I aim to specify in this treatment.

differences (this is reserved for a work focusing on types of political actors). However, one factor needs to be highlighted here that distinguishes public bureaucracies and business organisations from 'true voluntary associations'. This pertains to the role of the members' preferences in defining the goals and strategic choices of the authority field; that is, the extent to which the authority field is ideologically and operationally linked to the will of the members.

In public bureaucracies and business organisations the existence of a predefined goal, the attainment of which requires a high degree of cooperation and coordination among the members makes those members' preferences of little relevance in the definition of the goals and the strategic choices. Contracts that specify material rewards (salary, economic inducements, careers, etc.) in exchange for services link the members to the field but exclude them from participating in such decisions. True voluntary associations, on the contrary, are such exactly because people join as members to share in the goals and choices of the association. Although material incentives are not absent when it comes to administrative and leadership positions, most members are rewarded with their participation in the definition of the goals and strategies of the authority field. Such participation is not only permitted, but often facilitated, fostered and structured through specific mechanisms (assemblies, elections to leadership positions, debates, etc.). True associations qualify as such because of the fact that they are the expression of a spontaneous will of the members regarding their formation and preservation through consensus and solidarity. They are based on voluntary adhesion and a sharing of goals and resources. They are meant to increase the mobilisation of intents and the effectiveness of the instigations that define their mission. In the following discussion, I will mainly focus on the specificities of this latter kind of authority field.

Authority fields gather people together in order to create a group endowed with the capacity to multiply individual resources and efforts (see p. 97 for the special case of authority fields created by delegation from a superior authority). Authority fields are multipliers of individual capacities. The grouping of wills may take place with very selective incentives, such as profits and salaries in a firm or any other kind of 'club good' that is produced and reserved for the members of the authority field.[6] Of particular importance for us here are those assemblies of wills that aim to create a group endowed with the capacity to multiply some original request for behavioural compliance. This type of authority field is set up by means of a form of instigation that

---

6. Groups of individuals can create private associations (clubs) to provide themselves with non-rivalrous but small-scale goods and services that they can enjoy while excluding non-members from participation and consumption of the benefits. Buchanan, James M. (1965), 'An Economic Theory of Clubs', *Economica*, 32 (125), N.S., pp. 1–14.

specifically aims to multiply itself in order to behave as a team to exert pressure.

In most cases, therefore, authority fields are formidable multipliers of compliance requests. They aim to produce a compliance that is enhanced as compared to that attainable by personal means alone. Political entrepreneurs are active in setting up and nurturing authority fields for this purpose. However, if we admit the motivation of lust for command, political entrepreneurs may engage in this activity without being motivated by the multiplier effect for the rational pursuit of their goals. Instead, they may work as authority-seeking entrepreneurs, aiming to select those instigations that are more likely to allow them to mobilise supporters. In this case, the effect of multiplying compliance production is less important for the promoter than his achievement or consolidation of the command position. Therefore, a promoter exclusively or predominantly motivated by lust for command may be more prone to representing the preferences of the regular members than a promoter motivated by the multiplying effect in favour of his own preferences.

The presence of an authority for compliance production – sometimes with a complex articulated organisational structure comprising roles, competences and so on – should not mislead the observer. Every field of this kind tends to have a legal order that reflects its organisational and functional existence. This legal order is an element of the 'association', an aspect of its internal constitution. Although such an internal legal order can activate the group as a unitary actor in dealing with other actors, it does not 'create' any external order but only more or less effective pressures and requests for internal compliance. This is why any attempt to characterise the 'state', the 'political system', the 'political community' or any other kind of non-voluntary grouping as an associative order is misleading. The 'juridicity' of these groupings is not equivalent to the institutional dimension of a true association because the *societas* in them and under them does not constitute a voluntarily and therefore authentically constituted group. Whenever a legal order extends to encompass individual, composite or corporate actors that have not originally adhered voluntarily to the sharing of goals and resources, it can only be a manifestation of the power with which it was achieved, and the 'association' that results from it is purely fictitious.

Although authority fields are open fields like anarchic ones, the presence of command mechanisms introduces different opportunities for the production of compliance. Their more articulated organisational infrastructures, their multiplicity of roles, their complexity of rules constituting fields and defining their competences, their competition for authority positions and their possibility of open discussion of alternative instigations allow for more articulated mechanisms of compliance-seeking than is the case in anarchic fields. Some sanctioning is usually foreseen by the internal order of the field; persuasion is more articulated within its decision-making procedures; some conditioning is allowed by it having the same administration of the internal order and the decision-making process. In the end, however, the extent to which these resources can be used to act upon unwilling or opposing members is always a function of the cost of exit, so it is important to know whether alternative providers of similar functional authority exist or not.

In the case that alternative providers exist, there is a competition between authority fields providing similar goods/values (such as, for instance, political parties, firms and leisure associations). In the case that alternatives do not exist, exiting the field means renouncing those goods or values altogether. If there is only one National Tennis Federation controlling access to competitive tournaments, exiting (or being expelled from) that federation means you cannot play in official tournaments. Similarly, some professional associations, and in particular the registers of some accredited professions, assume the form of associations while in fact they uniquely administer professional credentials in a monopolistic way. The grey area that these 'corporative associative orders' or 'self-governments of categories'[7] introduce is only apparent. They usually 'govern' their interests with some kind of state facilitation, license or authorisation and implement some public policy function. Whatever level of autonomy is granted to them, they are delegated agencies of a governmental field. In general, however, the availability of alternative authority fields for similar goods/values modulates the cost of exit from each of them.

For those authority fields whose aim is the multiplication of requests for compliance, it is doubtful whether the actual reason for their formation is an original and continuing disposition of the individual participant to adhere. Problems of 'collective action' are seen as portentous obstacles to the constitution and survival of authority fields under certain assumptions about human nature.[8] In the absence of selective individual rewards, shared interests do not overcome individualistic calculations of convenience.[9] The dilemma of collective action is a powerful theoretical limiting condition. It

---

7. Streeck and Schmitter label these groups 'private interest government'. Streeck, W. and P. Schmitter (1985), 'Community, Market, State – and Associations? The Prospective Contribution of Interest Governance to Social Order', *European Sociological Review*, 1: 119–38, esp. p. 129.

8. In the light of the thesis in Olson, M. (1965), *The Logic of Collective Action. Public Goods and the Theory of Groups*, Cambridge, MA: Harvard University Press.

9. Assuming shared interests are not enough to overcome the individualistic calculus, it is interesting to ask whether shared fears are. You may share fear of a threat but not engage in collective action, assuming that others will do the job for you. On the contrary, one can argue that when physical integrity, life or liberty are at stake, the result of collective action may be significant even if the outcome is insignificantly affected by individual participation. On the other hand, at a certain point fear completely immobilises people. See the interesting discussion in Evrigenis, Ioannis (2008), *Fear of Enemies and Collective Action*, New York: Cambridge University Press, pp. 12–19.

is, however, somewhat fictitious to imagine that an authority field can arise and be sustained only by a mere encounter of self-determined and independent individual wills. It is difficult to imagine founding members having the same notion at the same time, meeting on common ground and coalescing naturally. Certain individuals take the initiative, very often motivated by the ambition to command, call others together and prevail on them to join in. Thus, at the inception of any authority field of this kind there are instigations and a request for compliance of some kind. The action of the initiators is driven by the image of things to do, goals to pursue or a project that for its fulfilment needs more forces than are available.[10] All groups of this sort arise out of a process of calls and responses.

No kind of authority field is a flat landscape of wills, therefore. They are always an irregular pyramid, with a tiny fraction of the associates in charge, not only of execution of the associative will but also of consciously reinventing it and inventing action for it. Beside this entrepreneurial group, the layered organisation of an authority field has a second circle 'which urges, criticises, pushes forward to the leading positions, and signals backwards to the greater number for their support'. Then a third layer exists that does not influence the leadership of the group but is conscious of the purpose pursued. Finally, the rest of the associated membership often has a confused and fitful perception of what it is all about.[11] An associated group of this kind is constantly in tension between the leaders executing a pre-existing will of the associates (for which no problem arises except that of their unfaithfulness) and elaborating the goals for the associates, thus continually regenerating the original incitation to adhere. Therefore, we should not portray the internal dynamics of an authority field as a simple confrontation between the associated wills, on the one hand, and the intentions of the leading representatives, on the other hand. We should instead observe the far more complex transactions of calls and responses through the layering of the association. Replicating a principal-agent model for any relation among the layers quickly leads to an unmanageable level of complication. To sum up, even if everywhere and always the few gather the energy of the many others, authority fields nevertheless remain 'open'. This openness, however, does not result merely from an instantaneous and continual evaluation/calculation of the costs and advantages of the associational goal but also from a mixture of the ambitions

---

10. See de Jouvenel, Bertrand (1959), *Authority: The Efficient Imperative*, in C. J. Friedrich (ed.), *Nomos I: Authority*, New York: New York University Press, reprinted in de Jouvenel (1992), *The Nature of Politics: Selected Essays of Bertrand de Jouvenel*, edited by Dennis Hale and Marc Landy, New Brunswick: Transaction, pp. 84–93.

11. De Jouvenel, Bertrand (1992; 1954), 'The Nature of Politics', in Dennis Hale and Marc Landy (eds.), *The Nature of Politics: Selected Essays of Bertrand de Jouvenel*, pp. 80–81.

of those in authority positions, a generation of ideas for action, ideological mobilisations of layers by superior ones, persuasion and manipulation efforts.

An additional important consideration that applies to authority fields is that their constitution is also the constitution of supra-individual actors who act in different fields. The primary leadership's rationale for constituting authority fields is to achieve the multiplication of wills that make their action more efficient in other fields, and namely in natural and governmental fields. When we observe the authority field in its own terms, it appears in its constitutive element of a gathering of wills. We focus on its internal ordering from the point of view of the layering of the associated wills and the internal interaction they give birth to. When we observe an authority field as a constituted composite actor, we see it in its relationships with other actors in different fields from the authority field, and namely in governmental and natural fields. The constitution of authority fields within predominantly natural fields constitutes the beginning of the dissolution of the natural fields. Authority fields constitute the most significant politically relevant actors that structure the interactions in governmental fields. It is, therefore, essential to underline the dual nature of authority fields as associations of wills and as potential composite actors.

However, the extent to which an authority field can constitute itself as a relevant actor in a different field depends on its constitutive element of the gathering of wills; that is, on its internal ordering. The possibility of conceiving of an authority field as a unified composite actor crucially depends on its capacity for strategic action. This capacity in turn depends on the varying degree of convergence/divergence of the cognitive maps and of the integration of preferences among the associates. This determines the field's capacity to forgo present satisfaction for future gains; to face some losses in order to obtain larger overall gains; to sacrifice and trade interests and preferences in one area to the advantage of interests and preferences in other areas; and to compensate losses to some members with gains to others (Kaldor optimality).[12] In the end, this means that the authority field's capacity for strategic collective action depends both on a convergence of preferences and on a capacity for internal conflict resolution within the field.

A further important reflection stems from the surprise of regarding, for instance, trade unions and political parties as authority fields. This somehow runs counter to common sense as they are commonly viewed as key political entities. However, the unorthodoxy of this view is only apparent. Intense struggles take place within political parties, but – from the analytical point of view – they are no different from the similar struggles that take place for leadership positions in sports, cultural or interest associations. The possibility

---

12. Scharpf, Fritz W. (1997), *Games Real Actors Play. Actor-Centered Institutionalism in Policy Research*, Boulder, CO: Westview Press, pp. 58–60.

that the field's members have of leaving the field with no or minimal costs makes the *internal dynamics* politically tenuous in the sense in which politics is defined here. It is only because parties, their leaders and their actions are *important in other fields* that we tend to see what happens within them as highly relevant politically. This begs the question of the difference between what is 'political' and what is 'politically relevant', which was touched upon in chapter 1 when reviewing different conceptions of politics. The view that everything that is politically relevant is by itself and by definition intrinsically 'political' fundamentally undermines any attempt to characterise the nuclear element of politics. It is insane to deny that many things that happen within political parties have consequences for other crucial aspects of the production of political compliance in a governmental field. It is equally insane to accept the principle that what is relevant for politics is in the 'political' category. As argued already, this would rapidly lead to untenable conclusions.[13] Being 'relevant to politics' does not define the category of the political. In turn, to deny that a given phenomenon has a high political intensity is not to claim that it is devoid of interest or relevance to politics.[14]

Natural fields

Natural fields are fields in which the actors are confined without the presence of a monopolisation of the production of conformity. In this case, the capacity of each actor to obtain the behavioural compliance of the others with his achieving his goals/values directly corresponds to the level of his own resources and to his skilful use of them. As actors find themselves in situations of resource asymmetry, promised recompenses or threats become the most typical means of achieving the compliance of the other actors. This is a compliance with the acquisition of specific goods and values, which, as in anarchic fields, is in no sense guaranteed but depends exclusively on resources and their strategic use through a continual process of conflict and negotiation. Political action, in this case, is action directed at others, aiming directly at their compliance with the actor's goals/values.

In the absence of other specific obligations among the actors, unilateral action tends to prevail as the basic orientation. Actors are constrained only

---

13. A further objection to this position is that the consequences of interactions in authority fields are political in the sense that they lead to consequences in the selection of personnel for public authorities or influence the policy choices of those same authorities. One can voluntarily exit authority fields, but one cannot exit the political consequences of the personnel or policy choices generated in them. My short answer here is that such external consequences do not directly derive from the internal dynamics of the authority field but from its more or less effectively behaving as an actor in another field, namely in a governmental field.

14. Mason, Andrew (1990), 'Politics and the State', *Political Studies*, 38: 575–87, esp. p. 579.

by physical and resource limitations and by the countermoves of the other actors. They may, in fact, communicate and reach agreements, but they are also free to violate them. In natural fields, actors interact in a context of non-cooperative games, by mutual adjustment,[15] negative coordination[16] and negotiation, particularly when agreements are self-executing and implementation is not a major problem. However, agreements that are more complex require more demanding institutional settings that reduce future uncertainty and the risk of opportunism.

Any actor achieves only the behavioural compliance of the others with his goals temporarily, and this heavily depends on the constellation of his personal resources and alliances with other actors. Changes in the quantity of resources or in their strategic value can modify pacts he has established. Alliances are unstable, with the result that acceptance, acquiescence and obedience are constantly at stake. This requires a constant input of resources into the field to maintain or modify the status quo. The compliance achieved is neither stable over time nor generalised. It is not stable because it often involves a transitory reunion to accomplish a particular purpose, which needs reviving on every occasion. In fact, the creation of durable cooperation based on a compliance relationship is unlikely to be very attractive for the actors affected. This may involve them in and commit them to a chain of actions that are ex ante unforeseeable and therefore eventually undesirable. Agreements and cooperation are difficult to extend into the future for different goals and purposes. The compliance that is achieved is also not guaranteed with respect to claims by all the other existing or potential actors in the field because they have no reason to recognise and respect either the compliance relation or the outcomes it leads to. The outcomes of the modalities of interaction described are inevitably precarious and unstable. They determine a situation of *uncertainty* (as to the costs and advantages) and also in extreme cases *insecurity* (as to physical integrity). For single actors, natural fields are uncertain and unsafe because the rules are not specified or do not exist to transform whatever behavioural conformity is achieved into a 'command'.

In natural fields, there is hardly any way to distinguish 'political' compliance specifically from any other kind of compliance. The action of man over man and the search for compliance do not have a specifically 'political' scope, but it is perhaps always 'political'. In principle, the lack of a specialised function of compliance production makes every claim for conformity as political as any other. In the unstable conditions and with the unstable

---

15. If we abandon full rationality and full information and we define a minimum level of bounded rationality. See Lindblom, C. (1965), *The Intelligence of Democracy: Decision Making through Mutual Adjustment*, New York: The Free Press.
16. Scharpf, *Games Real Actors Play*.

coalitions of the natural field, actors may 'politically' use any compliance achieved. Resources are primarily aimed at the maintenance of behavioural compliance, as concrete value directly depends on it. Final values are, in fact, merely acquired; they are *acquisitions* – more precisely, non-guaranteed and non-generalised acquisitions.

Governmental fields

A *governmental field* is a field in which the final goals/values guaranteed to any actor result from the role and function of a third actor (and its agents) located in a central hierarchy specialised in the production of behavioural compliance for the field. Governmental fields allow a further quantum leap in the form of political interactions. Politics takes on a definitely more familiar and routinised character. At the same time, it also introduces radically new problems that are unknown in other kinds of fields.

A field remains 'natural' as long as specific rules for the selection of 'commands' do not exist. In governmental fields, in the presence of competing requests for behavioural compliance, a process of selection takes place that transforms one of them into a form of 'command', successfully excluding the competing requests and stabilising the field.[17] The rules for the selection of the command specify and considerably reduce the means and resources that affect the selection of the command itself. In this sense, governmental fields *expand the scope of politics at the cost of its means*. The production of compliance is no longer achieved as an ad hoc result. It is not punctuated, uncertain or limited to a subset of the field's actors. It can be stabilised over time and generalised over a large set of actors.[18] This function is performed through the production of a number of key public goods. These are usually identified as *protection* (defence from others through coercive sanctions); *arbitration* (control and limitation of conflicts between qualified actors); *jurisdiction* (guarantees about compliance with commitments made by social actors and their respect for the services and performances promised and due); *regulation* (definition of the rules of the game); and *allocation* (direct allocation of goods, services and duties). While anarchic and authority fields are typically non-territorial membership spaces, and natural fields may be confined by any rule of closure (including territory), in governmental fields the typical form of confinement of actors is territorial. In this case, the monopolisation function takes an accentuated territoriality.

---

17. Note that in conformity with their nature this selection also exists in authority fields.
18. Stoppino puts a strong emphasis on the stabilisation and generalisation of the production of behavioural compliance. Stoppino, M. (1994), 'Che cosa è la politica', *Quaderni di Scienza Politica*, 1: 1–34.

Precisely because governmental fields stabilise and generalise the production of compliance – generating an environment that is in principle more stable, predictable and safe for the single actor – they also generate theoretically unsolvable predicaments.[19] First, in the process of constituting a governmental field, no rules or principles exist to define the territorial/membership boundary and the corresponding rules of exit and entry. The acts of confinement usually defining the original community find no convincing theoretical justification. A factually closed field generates problems for those who in principle would not be willing to stay in it, for those who would be willing to enter it and more generally for the rules to enlarge, restrict or otherwise modify the field's membership. In the factual constitution of a group, there is no known way of rationally defining or collectively deciding who should or should not be a member, who should constitute the political community. This constitutive predicament can be labelled the *membership predicament*.

Second, for any conceivable human group constituted as a governmental field, it is impossible to define the set of rules to be used to set those same rules. In other words, there are no rules to decide the rules for deciding. In one of his best pages, Bertrand de Jouvenel puts the problem as follows: Let us assume there is a specific problem concerning a decision to be taken. There will be disagreement about the concrete decision. Let us assume that there is agreement on the fact that the specific decision should be taken by resorting to some general principle and not 'arbitrarily' (in the sense of not dictated by principles). There will be disagreement about which principles to apply to the specific problem we want to solve by following principles. Let us assume that we have to agree on the procedure to select the general principle to solve the individual specific problem. There will be disagreement about how to select the procedure and so on.[20] Let us label this the *rule predicament*.

Finally, in governmental fields the question emerges of why people confined in the field should conform to the prevailing 'command'. Even if the definition of membership and the existence of rules for decisions are granted, there is no logical basis on which those who have not taken part in a concrete decision and/or when taking part have seen their desires unsatisfied should abide by them. It is easy to label this the *legitimacy predicament*. Analysis of legitimacy as the likelihood that 'collectivised' decisions – taken by somebody for somebody else – will be complied with by the somebody else in question even if the decisions are disliked and costly has proven to be empirically elusive. In this theoretical construction, legitimacy manifests its

---

19. I find Golding, William (1954), *Lord of the Flies*, London: Faber & Faber, a fascinating inquiry into primordial political predicaments.
20. De Jouvenel, Bertrand (1963), *The Myth of the Solution*, Addendum to *The Pure Theory of Politics*, p. 211.

crucial role only in extreme situations and usually can only be evaluated ex post. For this reason, most debates about 'legitimacy' concentrate on a more manageable definition that understands it as the principles and procedures by means of which it can be rationally argued that collectivised decisions must be accepted. This last definition is open to debate about legitimacy in the absence of hard evidence about the likelihood of obedience. Two solid consequences derive from this. First, legitimacy problems are minor, if not immaterial, whenever decisions are not collectivised; that is, when the actors concerned and affected are left with exit options – with the possibility of avoiding the application of decisions and their consequences. Second, legitimacy is equally unnecessary and immaterial when decisions are made with the direct participation of the actors that are concerned and affected – that is, when collectivised decisions are in fact collective decisions, when they are taken unanimously and actors have an effective veto over decisions they dislike. In short, legitimacy problems emerge only in conditions of confinement (no exit) and monopolisation (no unanimity). They only emerge and are crucially momentous in governmental fields.

In short, the constitution of every governmental field with external boundaries that set it apart from other entities, with rules to decide about rules and with an acceptable level of compliance with decisions, results from *acts* external to the territorial/membership group defined by these same principles. Any principle of constitutive decision-making (membership, rules or legitimacy) presupposes the constitution of the political formation by means different to those defined by the principle. Nothing can overcome this political principle of indeterminacy. Note that none of these predicaments is significant in non-governmental fields. The solution to the predicaments is a discontinuity of politics, for which we can find many ex post justifications but no ex ante foundation.

In this domain, political philosophy has for a long time been attempting to identify and justify the sources of political obligations. Why should individuals who are assumed to be free obey the law if they are not in fact compelled to do so? Articulate arguments, reasoning and justifications have been used in the attempt to find a rational and acceptable principle. We can underline the primitive facts of violence and coercion that constituted early communities and invoke the prudential acceptance of those in which we happen to be born. We can invoke the role of divinity in defining the original community worth constituting. It is possible to call upon 'constructed' and 'imagined' primordial communities of blood or kinship, language or culture. We can resort to the myth of an original contract among subjects. We can identify the state of nature with the form of some repeated game and conclude that under certain conditions individuals may agree to coerce each other to ensure cooperation and the optimal provision of 'collective goods'. One solution may be more convincing than another for any given moment and specific case, and certain solutions are clearly more historically sound than others are. However, the search proves elusive. We can admire the prudential principles that humanity has elaborated in certain historical periods and geographical areas to attenuate the indeterminacy and the risks and costs associated with governmental fields. Nevertheless, we cannot eliminate this indeterminacy. The three predicaments of politics are constantly sleeping under the embers of community life and may re-emerge in favourable circumstances. We can only constantly and pragmatically develop partial solutions to minimise the risks – which is indeed politics at its height.

The truth is that these predicaments owe their nature to the fact of having no solution. They are 'political problems' in the sense that no solution or response is adapted to the terms of the problems as they have been formulated. The fundamental predicaments are not solvable but can only be 'reformulated' in different terms to facilitate, at best, a pragmatic or compromise arrangement. Political problems may lead to accommodations, not to solutions.[21] Compromise, authority, agreement through reasoning and deliberation and so on can achieve accommodation. This accommodation is usually engendered in a process in which the obvious non-solvability of the political problem in its original formulation feeds back onto its initial terms, leading to a redefinition of the same problem in which the conditions to be satisfied are softened so as to make them more compatible. Usually, the shadow of authority can facilitate the softening of the conditions to be satisfied. However, for the primordial predicaments of the constitution of a governmental field, no 'shadow of authority' is available.

The constitutive dimensions of politics in governmental fields rest, therefore, on forms of factual imposition for the territorial or membership group. The constitutive predicaments of governmental politics can be solved only by an act of confinement of the actors that drastically reduces individual or aggregate exit options. In the end, the solution to political predicaments and the constitution of a governmental field is associated with a simple *factual* predominance of some mechanism to select the 'command' among the competing solicitations. It inexorably connects to the passage from the situation of multiple commands and multiple productions of compliance to a definition of the authority that emanates the decisive 'command'. In my view, this confirms that confinement and monopolisation are the grounding elements for different conditions of the political. The possibility of finding a *practical* solution to political predicaments depends on an institutional differentiation of the function of monopolistically providing compliance. Political

---

21. Ibid., pp. 207–8.

institutions and their properties are the key to the more or less satisfactory management of political predicaments.

In the realm of human interactions, *politics receives its special status by means of the particular nature of constitutive predicaments*. Politics is based on a series of constitutive aporias that are theoretically unsolvable, even though they are arguable and defensible. Such predicaments are absent in any other domain of human action. In these underlying indeterminate dimensions, 'politics' is the only sphere of human activity in which in every moment the foundations can be challenged, and agreements can be put at stake and violated with no formal or factual superior. Politics is that kind of human interaction in which the integrity of the membership or territorial group and the physical security of its members are constantly at stake. The field of constitutive predicaments of community life is the area in which 'politics' is most clearly foreign and irreducible to law. In any other subsequent circumstance, the politics of governmental fields closely connects with and links to law. Politics in governmental fields has no other goals and no other outcome than the structuring and restructuring of the rules and the institutions that constitute the underpinning of orderly living together. It is to be deplored that so much of contemporary political science has lost any anchorage to the most concrete manifestation of the political – the legal order. However, at the source of any legal order have always lain these constitutive predicaments for which no principle, rule, system of incentives or authority can be invoked, once they are challenged.[22]

TRANSITIONS

It is useful to underline again that the types of fields discussed here are archetypal forms to be used as analytical tools. They are not intended to exhaustively and exclusively classify the variety of concrete situations. They describe modalities of social interaction among actors and as such can be used to characterise concrete situations. The constitutive dimensions of confinement and monopolisation from which the types originate determine the

---

22. This vision contrasts with the rationalism of certain solutions to the predicaments of politics. Dealing with American federalist constitutionalism, Weingast defines a constitution – that is, the overcoming of political predicaments – in the following functional way: 'a constitution serves as a coordinating device, helping citizens to coordinate their strategy choices so that they can react in concert and police state behaviour'. Weingast, R. Barry (1995), 'The Economic Role of Political Institutions: Market-Preserving Federalism and Economic Development', *The Journal of Law, Economics and Organizations*, 11: 1–30, p. 11. In this account, the membership predicament is solved by fiat: the citizens. What they should be doing together is solved by an attribution of preferences: to police state behaviour and to protect economic rights. Why they should abide and obey is not a problem to the extent that citizens 'react in concert' and 'coordinate'.

nature of the final goals/values that compliance can yield, a topic dealt with in more detail in the next section. They also importantly shape individual actors' *orientations* (egoism, solidarity, etc.) and the predominant inter-actor *mode of interaction* (conflict, competition, negotiation, cooperation), topics that this book omits. Different fields can coexist or may be nested one inside another (see chapter 5).

In other words, the 'governmental field' is not the 'government' but a constellation of specific actors who are both confined and under a monopolistic provider of compliance. This social relation can be identified in many situations that we would not associate with traditional government structures and institutions. Similarly, there might be typical governmental structures and institutions that do not display the characteristics of a governmental field.

Let me give two examples to make my point clearer. In contemporary polyarchic polities, parliamentary committees and cabinets are at the core of the political system and are regarded as the main producers of collectivised decisions that are binding for the entire territorial group they impinge upon. They are uncontroversial instances of governmental institutions. However, these bodies should not necessarily be seen as 'governmental fields' in terms of the interactions that prevail among their members. Let us consider a multiparty coalition cabinet in an institutional structure that does not foresee any special dominance of the prime minister over the other ministers, not even that of primus inter pares. The members of the cabinet are either independent agents or agents of their respective political parties or factions. In both cases, their behaviour as cabinet members is independent of any single source of compliance production *within* the cabinet. They use their respective resources (blackmail potential, leadership skills or whatever else) to pursue decisions in line with their preferences in a continual process of negotiation and exchange that is constrained only by their calculations of the costs/advantages of keeping the coalition cabinet together or breaking it up. Such a cabinet would be best described analytically as an anarchic or natural field, with the consequences for compliance generation highlighted earlier, conspicuous among which are problems of coordination and collective action.

On the other hand, cabinets exist in which the prime minister enjoys considerable powers of agenda setting, coordination and programmatic guidance, up to the point of being able to appoint and dismiss individual ministers. Similarly, cases exist in which a single party dominates the cabinet, and its hierarchy constrains the behaviour of ministers to the point of effectively monopolising the production of compliance for the field. In these cases, the cabinet would be better viewed as an authority or a governmental field, depending on the concrete costs of exit individual ministers face.

The same considerations apply to parliamentary committees. These could similarly be flattened groups of independent MPs or organised by means of varying degrees of compliance monopolisation thanks to a seniority principle, the institutional prerogatives of the chair or the sheer discipline imposed by party alignments. Therefore, a cabinet – the quintessential institution of executive power – or a parliamentary committee – the quintessential institution of legislative power – can be characterised and analysed as different fields depending on the level of confinement of their members and the level of monopolisation of the production of compliance within them.

Therefore, transitions exist from one field to another for the same social relationship. These are among the most important transformations a social scientist can observe. In fact, transitions from one pure type to another are at the heart of families of key problems of political analysis. For instance, a generation of authority fields from within anarchic or natural field relationships implies that autonomous actors endowed with unilateral options may, under favourable conditions, cooperate and establish forms of associational authority and/or self-governance in specific areas, notwithstanding the fundamentally open nature of the fields. These transitions tap the problems identified by collective action and social dilemma theories. A transition from an anarchic to a natural field takes place whenever processes of actor confinement are successful, whatever the basis for such confinement. Such a transition focuses on 'confinement' as a constitutive aspect of the most significant political interactions. On the contrary, processes of actor de-confinement preside over transitions from governmental fields to authority fields and from natural fields to anarchic ones.

Transitions from natural to governmental fields occur through processes of monopolisation that result from conflicts among alternative potential providers of behavioural compliance. Such transitions accompany the generation and satisfactory institutional solution of constitutive predicaments – regarding membership, rules and legitimacy. A transition from an authority to a governmental field presupposes that the monopoliser of the authority field successfully manages to prevent the members from exiting and therefore increases his capacity to extend his rule from the originally functionally defined field of interaction to other spheres.

Governmental fields may collapse into natural ones whenever the monopoliser loses his position and faces competition from alternative monopolisers. Moreover, decisions by a governmental field's rulers may 'naturalise' spheres of relationships previously under their direct rule. Transitions from governmental to anarchic fields involve an explicit (either forced or spontaneous) withdrawal of the monopoliser of compliance production from a specific social relationship (such as when the ruler de-regulates or renounces the regulation of specific fields). Similarly, a governmental ruler may foster the formation of authority fields by delegating some governmental competence with the aim of overcoming collective action problems. Authority fields can dissolve into less authoritative environments of anarchic or natural fields whenever the monopolistic provider of the field fails to maintain the 'meeting of wills' that originally constituted his or her authority.

Each of these main transitions identifies, therefore, a definite set of core theoretical problems. A considerable proportion of unfolding political processes can be profitably defined, or redefined, according to these analytical categories.

TYPES OF REQUEST FOR COMPLIANCE AND TYPES OF FINAL VALUES

In chapter 2, I argued that any request for compliance is intrinsically political but that the degree or intensity of the 'politicalness' varies depending on the conditions. These conditions define the *type of compliance* on which the final values depend, on the one hand, and the *nature of the final values* achieved, on the other.

I begin with a more accurate definition of the different types of compliance already mentioned in the text. Let A be the actor who requires compliance and B the actor to whom the request is addressed.

In terms of *voluntariness*, the compliance actor A can achieve from B with his final values can be either

- *willing* or
- *forced*.

We have already seen how difficult this distinction can be, particularly in the case of anticipated reactions, but also in many other grey areas.

In terms of *stability*, compliance can be either

- *occasional*, and therefore in need of continual regeneration, or
- *stabilised*, in the sense of enduring over time with no (or little) effort to continually generate and maintain it.

In terms of *scope*, compliance can be either

- *circumscribed* around the actors involved in specific social interactions (A and B in the simplified case) or
- *generalised*, that is, extended over the entire (membership or territorial) group (A and B and also all the other actors in the field).

In terms of its *source*, compliance can be either

- *personalised*, to the extent that it depends on the specific 'qualities' and individual resources possessed by A and B and on their personal direct relationship, or
- *institutionalised*, depending of the roles, competences, rights and duties which pertain to certain positions, and therefore independent of the direct relationship between A and B.

For the sake of analytical simplification, in this book I have assumed a single and undifferentiated 'ruler' or 'monopoliser' (RU); that is, I have not tackled questions related to institutional differentiations of rulership, and I have not discussed 'political institutions'.[23] This leads to a somewhat less important role at this stage for the third dimension of compliance production differentiation – that between personalised and institutionalised compliance. Here, I focus primarily on the dimensions of stability and generalisation.

By 'the nature of the final values' I do not mean what these final values concretely are (cars, legislation, company shares or positions) but *the mechanism for their achievement, the title with which they have been obtained*. In my perspective, the nature of the final values depends on the type of behavioural compliance on which they rest, which is in turn highly dependent on the field of interaction.

In *anarchic fields*, requests for compliance are by definition not supported by the possibility of making available or withdrawing some form of resource (RE: material, symbolic and so forth). All A's mundane requests for help, favour, support, aid and so on risk the possibility of B exiting the social relationship, with it being impossible for A to prevent it. Note that the lack of possibility of supporting a request with resources is not due to A lacking resources relevant to B. These may exist, but they cannot weigh on B's choice given his freedom to leave the relationship. Note also that this does not mean that A's request will inevitably meet with a refusal or a non-response. There are plenty of reasons why B may agree to acquiesce: love, sympathy, reciprocity, conventions or social norms and so on. It only means that, whatever the response, it will only depend on the autonomous disposition of B towards A or her request. Strictly speaking, therefore, one could even doubt whether the idea of 'compliance' is an adequate concept for this kind of social relationship field. *In anarchic fields, resources can only be exchanged; actors may use resources to obtain values, but cannot use them to achieve compliance.* Mutual agreement is the dominant mode of interaction, characterised

---

23. A theory of political institutions resting on compliance seeking political action needs a separate treatment.

by spontaneous, voluntary and self-enforcing agreements among parties. It will result in final values that take the form of mere *synallagmatic exchanges* in which individuals reciprocally obligate or sympathetically respond. This world of synallagmatic relations assumes reciprocal commitments, and agreements arrived at in this way can only be valid for the parties who have achieved them. They can be neither 'generalised' to other members of the field – and thereby be protected from interventions by other actors – nor 'stabilised' over time. They need to be continually regenerated. The final values are therefore achieved by using resources as exchange instruments in this typical form:

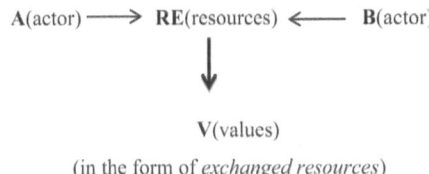

(in the form of *exchanged resources*)

In natural fields, given that B cannot escape the relationship, compliance can be sought by means of resources that A has that are relevant to B, in the absence of which B would be free to determine her response autonomously. A directly operates on B, in the sense that threats and inducements by A directly affect B. The request is punctuated and in principle depends on a skilful use of resource asymmetries among actors. It is conceivable that the resource asymmetries are so large and stable over time that the compliance achieved through their use acquires some degree of stabilisation. Many actors in the field can come to recognise this systematic and permanent compliance production and accept it or anticipate its possible use. It remains nevertheless clear that this 'power' always rests on the actors' resources (or on alliances and coalitions of actors), and it is subject to radical modifications depending on changes in such resources used for sanctioning, conditioning and persuading. Therefore, the compliance produced cannot be generalised to extend to all the members of the field but is limited to the parties in an action. Nothing guarantees that the compliance so achieved in a specific case is maintained over time with any degree of certainty. There is no certainty that A will again have the resources necessary or that B will again lack alternative resources with which to resist. The compliance achieved in this contest is occasional, punctuated and limited in scope to the actors involved. Under these conditions, the final values achieved are clearly not 'exchanged values', but rather 'acquired values'. In this case, final values are mere *acquisitions* because of the conditions of compliance under which they have been obtained. The final values are therefore achieved by using resources to generate compliance, and the typical scheme runs from actors (A) and their resources (RE) directed at B in the form of a request for compliance (C) with the final values (V) in the form of acquisitions.

$A \rightarrow RE \rightarrow B \rightarrow C \rightarrow V$ (final values in the form of *acquisitions*)

In *authority fields* (and in governmental fields), requests for compliance and final values radically change. *Requests no longer flow from A to B* with a view to achieving her punctuated compliance with specific acquisitions by means of resources. The presence of a monopolistic provider of compliance means that A does not need to act directly on B, bringing his resources to bear on her. Requests and instigations address the monopolistic provider with the aim of achieving compliance by B through its *command*. This command rarely takes the form of a direct power of A over B. It will typically be a more general rule, which will therefore be generalised for the entire membership of the field and stabilised over time, at least until a further command modifies it. Due to the absence of any direct action by A on B, compliance production is already de-personalised and institutionalised.

In the passage from anarchic and natural fields to authority fields, the nature of the resource used to sustain requests fundamentally alters. *Given that A does not address B directly, the resources that sustain his request are no longer resources relevant to B but rather resources relevant to the ruler (RU)*. They are usually specified and predefined by the internal ordering (the institutions) of the authority field and take the specific form of *support for/ opposition to RU*. A's request is therefore based on the capacity to withdraw or make available the specific support the monopolistic provider needs to retain its position.

The compliance thus obtained is stabilised over time and generalised to the entire membership of the field. However, it cannot extend beyond the membership group that defines the authority field. The possibility of all actors, including the hypothetical B we use in these examples, exiting the field guarantees that the behavioural compliance produced by RU cannot extend beyond the functional scope for which the field was voluntarily constituted. Exiting the field automatically means discharging oneself from the commitments, duties and rights that characterise it. This may entail some costs (which will largely depend on the availability of other fields able to offer the same or similar final values), but it must remain a feasible option for the analytical definition of the field. The final goods or values achieved within such a field are therefore neither voluntary exchanges nor mere punctuated acquisitions that A can get from B, as in anarchic or natural fields. I label this type of final values, which are functionally circumscribed and open to voluntary discharge, *endowments*. There is no intrinsic lexicographic value in the term 'endowment'. I use it instrumentally to identify the specific analytical nature of this type of final value. The typical scheme runs from actor (A) and his specific support resources (SU) towards the ruler (RU) to the request for compliance C and to the final values (V), this time in the form of endowments. B is absent from this process, unless, of course, she advances a different injunction to RU opposed to that of A.

A → SU → RU → C → V (final values in the form of *endowments* within the membership group)

Most of what has been said earlier for authority fields also applies to governmental fields. Even in governmental fields, requests for compliance are addressed to RU, not to other actors. In this case too, therefore, the resources that sustain requests are not A's resources relevant to B. They pertain to A's capacity to positively or negatively affect the ruler. The possibility of giving or withdrawing support to groups and factions in the political class in the specific struggle for public authority sustains the request. Institutions define the resources permitted. There is no need, and little possibility, to continually accumulate resources to feed a similarly continual process generating B's compliance. Also in this case, the output from the ruler takes the form of a generalised and stabilised command. The crucial difference, however, is that no actor in the governmental field can exit the field with low or limited costs. A command generalised for a closed field has the typical property of erga omnes validity. Enforcement is left to the specialised third party, and actors do not need to directly engage in the enforcement process but can at most be required to 'appeal' to the enforcer. This means that, in principle, there are no limits to the kind and scope of values that this type of command can achieve.

The final values A can achieve as a result of this type of command are neither values exchanged with B nor acquisitions directly obtained from B, and not even endowments valid within the field to which both A and B belong. They take the form of a 'guaranteed right' for A, which is valid for all the members of the group, and their membership is not voluntary. The request by A, therefore, aims at the modification of the distribution of conferred and guaranteed rights *within the entire closed field*. To refer to this type of final value and to mark the difference from synallagmatic exchanges, acquisitions and endowments, I use the term 'entitlement' (see chapter 5 for a more extended discussion). Entitlements are conferred guaranteed rights over final values stabilised and generalised over a non-voluntary and closed field. The form of the connection between the actor and the final values remains similar to that of the authority field but for the previously mentioned nature of the final value:

A → SU → RU → C → V (final values in the form of *entitlements* or guaranteed rights within the territorial group)

In *governmental* (and authority) fields, the presence of political institutions (which in this treatment I identify with the ruler) considerably changes the picture. Institutions eliminate the need for any given actor A to accumulate general resources to obtain compliance. With institutions, the achievement of A's final values passes directly through conformity by B without any apparent use of resources that A has that are relevant to B. In this sense and in this context, institutions as a framework for prescribed behaviours constitute constraints on an individual's behavioural choices that do not derive from the use of another individual's resources. A 'rule' is an institutional request for behavioural compliance claiming guaranteed conformity from all the other actors in the field.

As territory is a predominant feature of the governmental field, the compliance that is produced extends its scope to the territorial group (reducing the exit options of all sorts of actors, individuals, associations, corporations, territories, etc.). Its generalisation is therefore maximum and in principle

Table 4.1. Fields by type of actors, compliance and final values

Fields	Type of actors	Type of behavioural compliance	Type of final values
Anarchic fields	Actors with unilateral action options, including exit	Non-protected, non-stabilised, non-generalised voluntary compliance	*Synallagmatic exchanges* reciprocal commitment between A and B
Natural fields	Confined actors with unilateral action options	Punctuated compliance, rarely stabilised, non-generalised	*Acquisitions* action of A over B
Authority fields	Actors bounded by voluntarily constituted fields	Compliance generalised and stabilised only within the membership group	*Endowments* confined rights action of A towards RU
Governmental fields	Actors in territorially bounded fields	Compliance stabilised and generalised for the entire territorial group	*Entitlements* guaranteed rights action of A towards RU

encompasses at least potentially any other kind of field that happens to exist on a given territory. Within its territorial scope the governmental field therefore has, at least in principle, the capacity to define the nature of all other fields, depending on the circumstances.

Table 4.1 summarises the argument of this chapter. The correspondence between the different types of field, the actors' options, the types of compliance production and the nature of the final values achieved is only sharp in an analytical ideal-typical treatment. Grey areas and hybrid situations can easily be identified which make the analysis more problematic. In any concrete field characterised by confinement and monopolisation features, special moments, specific situations and niches of relationships exist that do not neatly reproduce the dominant type. In particular, in almost any authority or governmental field one can identify anarchic or natural spheres of relationships. However, the analytical scheme even has the capacity to disentangle complex, mixed or hybrid situations. I claim that when we identify a specific instance of a relationship through the core features of confinement and monopolisation, the logic of the type of compliance and of final value attainment stringently deploys itself. Logical consequences and precise hypotheses can follow concerning the main dynamics of the political process. These concern:

(1) actors' orientations,
(2) modes of interaction,
(3) conflict resolution capacities,
(4) negative externalities,
(5) welfare consequences and
(6) legitimation problems.

Chapter 5

What is 'politics'?

In the previous chapters, I have defined the nature of elementary political action and how it deploys itself in different fields characterised by different levels of actor confinement and monopolisation of command. The ways political action achieves its final values also vary from field to field, depending on the type of compliance: voluntary or imposed, occasional or durable, circumscribed or extended, personalised or institutionalised. The resources that individual and composite actors utilise also vary from field to field: actors' own resources versus actors' support for actual or potential rulers. The nature of the final values is different in different fields: synallagmatic exchanges as reciprocal commitments, acquisitions as action by A over B, endowments as confined rights and entitlements as guaranteed rights.

It is time to revert to the question posed in chapter 1 – what is politics? – and see whether the arguments in chapters 2–4 result in any advances. I move from nuclear political action to a general characterisation of 'politics'. I establish a close isomorphic relationship between nuclear political action as a request for compliance and politics as the production of that special type of compliance that is imposed, generalised, stabilised and institutionalised. While political action characterises all fields of social relationship, politics as a regular and stable production of compliance can take place only in authority and, above all, in governmental fields. However, I do not engage in a separate treatment of authority and governmental fields. I have amply elaborated the key difference between them, and its implications for political production readily ensue. This chapter is concerned with the politics of governmental fields.

THE POLITICAL 'GOOD'

Discussion of the production function of the governmental field leads us to tackle the approach mentioned in the introduction that defines the political through what it produces, through its output, through the final values that it distributes.

At first sight, the answer is elementary. The political process in the governmental field produces steady outputs in the form of *regulations*, which prescribe or proscribe conduct, calibrate incentives and allocate responsibilities; *allocations*, in the form of amounts due, services, welfare provisions and so on; *jurisdiction*, which provides access to the legal regulation of conflicts and conflicting rights; *arbitration*, in the form of management of internal conflict among politically relevant actors (to the extent that it is not left to jurisdictional interventions); and *protection* against aggression and violations. However, a closer inspection clarifies that these factual outputs are the obvious but not the decisive production of the political. When the aforementioned outputs define the essence of the political process, politics appears as a production process very much like the economic production process. The emphasis is on the production of collective goods, detected from the nature of their provider and labelled 'authoritatively produced goods'. Regulations, allocations, jurisdiction, arbitration and protection are goods, much as cars, clothes and insurance are (private) goods produced through a differently organised production process.

Politics conceived as an 'authoritative' allocation of values/goods can be compared with other non-authoritative mechanisms of allocation. The discussion focuses on whether certain values/goods are obtained more or less 'efficiently' if they are distributed 'authoritatively', by an 'author' who enjoys authority, or via negotiated agreements or mere acquisitions. This perspective sees authority, hierarchy and politics in functional terms, as the result of specific and particular circumstances in which negotiated agreements (improperly labelled 'contractual relations', see pp. 120–21), regarded as the paradigm of all sort of social interactions, fail to deliver certain kinds of good. The emergence of a hierarchy (and the development of organisations) results from 'market failure'.[1] Politics so conceived is exogenous to and extraneous from the economic realm and is a more or less efficient complement or service to it. When this servicing extends beyond these efficiency necessities, it damages the economic tendency to generate efficiency and generates political

---

1. I take the work of Williamson as representative of this predominant view of politics by economists; Williamson, Oliver (1975), *Markets and Hierarchies, Analysis and Anti-Trust Implications*, New York: The Free Press. Peter Blau tends to give equal weight to political power and exchange. See Blau, Peter (1964), *Exchange and Power in Social Life*, New York: Wiley & Sons.

'rent seeking' such as illegitimate acquisitions of values/goods that should have been sought differently.[2]

To a large extent, this understanding of politics is a new version of the historical opposition in political thought between two equal obligations, political obligations, on the one hand,[3] and private obligations, on the other, often identified with contracts. This opposition more or less summarises all the related dichotomies of state/society, status/contract, community/society and so forth in political theory, and clashes between two supposedly equal obligations have often transformed themselves into unsolvable antagonisms. Oscillations between the prevalence of one or the other have marked oscillations in regimes and political systems over time with a vision in which an enlargement of one area corresponds to a shrinking of the other: enlargement of political obligations reduces the area of private obligations, and vice versa.

This perspective also evidences a renewed effort to reduce the political to the contract. In the history of modern political thought, there have been continual attempts to uphold the idea that the private obligation is somehow natural and should prevail over the artificiality of the political obligation. The latter is best characterised as an ancillary derivation from the private obligation. Hume defined 'stability of possession, of its transference by consent, and of performance of promises' as the 'three fundamental laws of nature'.[4] It is, therefore, not surprising that situations not characterised in a strictly juridical sense (such as political obligations) continue to be represented as analogous to the image of constraints that is typical of the civil (or statutory) institution of private obligations. This is an attempt to nullify the difference

---

2. The origin of this view is Adam Smith's theory of the 'hidden hand' that performs far better than any authority-based mechanism of allocation. In his words, 'Every individual is continually exerting himself to find out the most advantageous employment for whatever capital he can command. It is his own advantage, indeed, and not that of the society, which he has in view. But the study of his own advantage naturally, or rather necessarily, leads him to prefer that employment which is most advantageous to the society'. Smith, Adam (1776; 1910), *The Wealth of Nations*, 2 vols., London: J.M. Dent and Sons, vol. 1, p. 398. However, in a less famous and certainly less frequently quoted passage Smith required the state to carry out specific tasks to allow this advantage of self-regulating individual interactions: 'First, the duty of protecting society from the violence and invasion of other independent societies; secondly, the duty of protecting ... every member of the society from the injustice or oppression of every other member of it ... and, thirdly, of erecting and maintaining certain public works and certain public institutions which it can never be for the interest of any individual ... to erect and maintain; because the profit could never repay the expenses to any individual'. Ibid., vol. 2, pp. 180–81. This is an impressive list of tasks for public authorities to carry out. It is surprising that these tasks are regarded as 'technical' tasks in that they provide infrastructural support to the beneficial enterprise of self-regulating synallagmatic relationships in which public authorities should not interfere – a point noted in Stepan, Alfred (1978), *The State and Society. Peru in Comparative Perspective*, Princeton: Princeton University Press, p. 9.

3. The term *political obligation* is likely to have been first used in Green, Thomas (1885–1888), 'Lectures on the Principles of Political Obligation', in R.L. Nettleship (ed.) (1986), *Works*, 3 vols., London: Longman; Cambridge University Press.

4. Hume, David (1739–1740; 1978), *A Treatise of Human Nature*, Oxford: Clarendon Press, p. 526.

between a 'contractual' relationship and a command/obedience relationship, between a bond deriving from a principle of reciprocity (or of redrafting) and one which is irreducible to the claims of the parties involved. This vision dominates economic theories of politics today, and increasingly theories of politics tout court. However, it generates several distortions in the understanding of the good(s) politics produces.

Much as the economic production process is inadequately described in functional terms – by the final values that it eventually provides to individuals – similarly we can doubt that political production can be defined along similar functional lines by simply changing the nature of the final values. The final values produced by the economic process are the unintentional result of individual and corporate appetites for profit. Similarly, in politics the production of public goods should be regarded as the unintentional result of the intersection between motivational drives constituted by the appetite for authority of those engaged in the struggle for it and by the appetite for concrete final values – similar to cars, clothes and insurance – of politically relevant actors and ordinary citizens. Values produced authoritatively are values produced by public authorities, but their authoritativeness does not come merely from this. Authoritativeness ultimately means that they are allocated through 'binding decisions', decisions that are valid for every member of a territorial/membership group and that are enforced, adjudicated and defended by the unique resources of the ruler with a view to guaranteeing generalised and stabilised compliance. But if the political production process is the unintended result of the appetites for command of factions competing for public authority and the appetite for final goods of ordinary actors, it cannot be seen as rationally driven by or instrumentally resulting from an understanding of market failures. Why should factions competing for government positions, politically relevant actors or even ordinary citizens confine their ambitions to such a benign redressing of market failures?

If we focus on synallagmatic relations among individuals in their pure form, they can offer some guarantees against a number of uncertainties concerning non-delivery, incompleteness or explicit violation of the terms of agreements, but this insurance is limited to the partners in the specific relation. Acquiring something, in whatever way the 'acquisition' takes place, is not the same thing as seeing your right to that acquisition accepted and respected by all the relevant actors in a field, that is, as transforming the acquisition into an 'entitlement'. Private dealings on the market may give you a car in exchange for a price, but nothing guarantees that all the other actors not involved in the specific transaction will respect your right to possession, that is, your right to exclude others from using the good acquired. No agreement, however complete and well specified, can cover the risks of non-compliance with your acquisition by the entire membership of the field. If any synallagmatic deal among private persons required acceptance by all the other members of the field, it would generate unbearable transaction costs. What we commonly label 'contracts' – as opposed to synallagmatic dealings – do not include a clause stating that they should also be respected by all those who have not signed them. This goes without saying. Still, the 'without saying' is telling. There must be an implicit guarantee that such contracts will be accepted and respected by all those who are extraneous to them. It could be argued that such contracts deserve respect because they exchange values over which property rights are established. However, these property rights are other contracts, the validity of which also needs to extend to the entire membership of the field. How can such a warranty emerge for all the other members of a large social field?

In my view, this suggests that the core of political production is not the allocation of a special kind of values defined as different in nature because they are 'authoritatively' produced rather than 'privately' produced. Instead, the core lies in the *warranty* that everybody else will respect the allocation. This warranty – let us call it a *political warranty* – is therefore not typical of a special type of values (those allocated authoritatively) but of all types of allocations, including therefore those that result from synallagmatic relations, which we can properly call 'contracts' precisely to the extent that they incorporate this warranty. From this point of view, there is no difference between buying a car and obtaining a favourable regulation. Both depend on the same 'political warranty' that generalises and stabilises the acquisition *beyond the partners involved*. No skilfully devised system of incentives and disincentives among contracting partners can achieve this warranty. Synallagmatic exchanges produce only acquisitions (possessions) that turn into entitlements thanks to the effect of the political warranty. This is why the generalised use of the term 'contract' is misleading, and throughout this text I prefer the term 'synallagmatic relations' to denote exchanges that, in their pure form, lack such a warranty. In our conventional understanding, the term 'contract' already includes and incorporates a political warranty and generates the impression that property rights over what can be exchanged exist *ab imis*, are different from authoritative allocations and in the end are the basis from which individuals generate authority.[5]

In the most advanced forms of the governmental field, the essence of the political is a production and distribution of mutual guarantees among a large

---

5. Williamson, again, best epitomises this view: 'in the beginning there were markets'; Williamson, Oliver E. (1975), *Markets and Hierarchies, Analysis and Anti-Trust Implications: A Study in the Economics of Internal Organizations*, New York: The Free Press, p. 20. In his view, private property and markets can emerge through 'private orderings', that is, through synallagmatic transactions between individuals without any 'state' interference; Williamson, Oliver E. (1983), 'Credible Commitments: Using Hostages to Support Exchange', *American Economic Review*, 74: 519–40.

set of actors. Leaving the production of certain values/goods to private dealings does not mean that they are without a warranty. Seeing politics as the functional residual of synallagmatic relations is, therefore, a devastating optical distortion, at both the empirical and normative levels. Therefore, if politics is not a different production function for specific values, I conclude that it produces a *single value/good*: a web of reciprocal guaranteed rights among the members of an extended membership or territorial group. The political process does not produce values allocated in a special way (authoritatively public as opposed to synallagmatic-private) but values that incorporate a special warranty, which is required for both 'private' and 'public goods'.

Let us restate this main conclusion by quickly recalling the argument about the nature of final values for citizens and politically relevant actors. In anarchic and natural fields, actors seek values through the direct utilisation of their resources in dealings with others. These acquisitions do not have a permanent extended guarantee that others will comply with them, except on an occasional and accidental basis. In governmental fields, it is no longer necessary to achieve the compliance of others with your securing of final values through direct political action. Any single actor no longer needs to accumulate a variety of personal resources or to continually invest them in the generation of specific and punctuated behavioural compliance by others with respect to the values and goals she pursues. Instead, she can seek such compliance through the distribution function of the political hierarchy. Therefore, values and goals change their nature: instead of directly acquired goods, they become *entitlements* guaranteed by the public authority. In a governmental field, individual resources are directed towards acquisitions of 'entitlements', not of values or goods. The prototypical example of this transformation of acquisitions into entitlements is indeed the historical development of property rights. Usually, holders of important resources such as property and wealth accept being completely unarmed – and therefore renounce defending their values through a direct use of their own resources – only when the monopoliser of compliance production demonstrates its commitment and ability to provide such protection.[6]

I long hesitated in selecting the term *entitlement*. 'Entitlements' include familiar things: services, competences, liberties, faculties and capacities,[7] titles, goods and credentials *as guaranteed by public authorities*. The term covers common things such as recognition of the faculty to exercise a profession or to possess a good, authorisation to sell alcohol or build a wall in your garden, regulations on producing milk, access to national health services and so on. It roughly corresponds to what Stoppino labels 'guaranteed powers'; it

---

6. Winters, Jeffrey (2011), *Oligarchy*, Cambridge: Cambridge University Press, p. 33.
7. Including, therefore, civic and political 'rights'.

has some similarity with what Hart identifies as 'conferred powers';[8] and with a different emphasis it points to the many definitions that underline the 'binding' and 'collectivised' decisions that sustain them. I eventually chose the term 'entitlement' because it highlights what I am particularly interested in underlining: *the nature of the title* to the acquisition of final values. The term 'entitlement' conveys the idea that these concrete goods and values, whether they are distributed by the public authority or achieved through private dealings, have a crucial string attached to their concreteness: a guaranteed quota of compliance, a specific 'political warranty'. What matters is not exclusively the capacity to sell tobacco or to build a wall but the warranty guaranteeing the positive disposition of others towards your exercise of this capacity. Similarly, what matters is not (only) your specific deal (the 'exchange') with the car salesperson but (also) *the positive disposition of all other field members towards this deal*. The fact that this 'positive disposition of the others' is not formally the object of the deal between the parties and it is not specified in it conceals the very nature of the political warranty that subtends every synallagmatic relation. The distinction of 'public' versus 'private' goods is therefore immaterial with respect to the political warranty, which sustains both.

The fact that exchanges and acquisitions, on the one hand, and endowments and entitlements, on the other, have the same factual form conceals the crucial difference. In both cases you may aim to build a wall along the border of your garden. You may force your neighbour – possibly the only person who perceives and cares about your request – to accept it thanks to your skills and resources. In this case, your political action is oriented directly towards achieving his behavioural compliance with your goal, a compliance that does not extend beyond the restricted circle of those directly forced into acquiescence. But you may also seek an entitlement, a guaranteed right to build the wall, which can only be granted by the ruler. In this second case, you simply ignore the neighbours because you aim at a guaranteed right that shelters you from their counteractions, as well as from those of any other actor in the field.

Therefore, an 'entitlement' is not defined through its concrete factuality but through its more abstract quality of being a guarantee, of incorporating a quota of compliance. Through its protection, arbitration, jurisdiction, regulation and allocation activities a governmental field does not distribute values, goods and so on but distributes guarantees in the form of just claims or prerogatives. An entitlement represents a capacity to enjoy a good, perform an activity, have a competence and so on *with respect to which the dispositions and attitudes to compliance of all the other actors are fixed and stabilised in time*. In this sense, the role of politics in governmental fields is to produce

---

8. Hart, H. L. A. (1961; 1994, 2nd ed.), *The Concept of Law*, Oxford: Clarendon, p. 48.

a due share of compliance for everybody. 'Authoritativeness' refers to, embodies and is constituted by nothing else than the effect of a generalised and stabilised quota of behavioural compliance. The political output of a governmental field is a network of binding decisions and rules from which actors cannot escape. The key feature, however, is not the binding decisions per se but rather the creation of a guaranteed multilateral compliance for a vast group of actors.[9]

The network of multilateral guaranteed compliances that entitlements produce makes it possible for a plurality of actors to engage in relevant social interactions such as negotiations, competition, cooperation and limited conflict. The assumption is that no actor is free to endanger the network of compliance except via the further production and modification of entitlements. The legal system is the embodiment of a mutual recognition of the right of others to a quota of guaranteed compliance, but the setting up of the legal order, modification of it and actors' confinement and de-confinement strategies that are pursued *through* the legal order have no or very limited legal foundations. The legal system does not generate guaranteed rights. When it works properly, it is a means of precisely defining them and a credible commitment to defending them. Of course, legal adjudication is often about eligibility to entitlement and has considerable implications in this regard, which are often unforeseen by the producers of the guaranteed rights. Human rights, economic rights and more generally the 'constitutionalisation' of specific rights may considerably circumscribe, predefine or limit the scope of political action in specific circumstances. However, it remains true that political action can thaw any frozen right and revise any constitutionalisation of specific rights. Law does not produce entitlements; it manages them.

Reasoning *a contrario* demonstrates the identification of politics with the extended political warranty. Situations in which this single good is not produced best evidence its nature. The more or less extended nature of the political production function of collective goods creates no problem for the definition of the political. We can produce or not produce social rights, clean gardens and efficient public schooling, but when politics fails to deliver the essential good of a stabilised and generalised web of guaranteed rights for the entire field, and the governmental field hence slides into a natural one, then we observe a total collapse of all other specific goods, both *private and public*. In a situation of 'market failure', we may witness a more or less extended and efficient production of public goods; it is only in the case of 'politics failure' that we recognise the essence of political production.

---

9. Stoppino, *Potere e teoria politica*, p. 245.

At this stage, a general definition of politics emphasises the production (challenge, destruction) of generalised and stabilised guaranteed rights for an entire field that has overcome political predicaments. Both competition for public authority and searches for specific entitlements granted by authority are therefore 'political'.[10] Consequently, in governmental fields, it is impossible to identify a *single* motivational goal behind political action, and this is perhaps why a motivational approach to political action is rarely considered. While for the first type of actors (competing subgroups among the political class) politics has the motivation of obtaining, maintaining or accruing the sources of their claims for public authority, for other politically relevant actors and for ordinary citizens political action is mainly individual or collective pressure for entitlements. Entitlements are what common citizens and politically relevant actors want, and they tend to judge the struggle for political authority from this point of view. This quest is sustained by the specific resource that is able to affect the factions of the political class in competition for public authority, which is 'support' (or no support) in the specific form that the historical circumstances make significant. A definition of politics as competition to win public authority (political power) alone is insufficient, because it leaves out the other half of politics represented by ordinary actors' searches for entitlements from public authorities. A characterisation of politics that emphasises the mere allocation of values/goods is unsatisfactory because it confuses the factual outcome – goods, values and so on – with the specific 'political' weight that is added to them by the political warranty. Moreover, this characterisation obscures the competition for political authority among potential leaders and their followers under the assumption that this competition is oriented towards allocating values.

The political good: Power, public goods and social dilemmas

In this section, I intend to continue to elaborate on the idea of the 'political warranty' or 'political good' with direct reference to three alternative views of the political: politics as power, politics as public good production and politics as the solution to social dilemmas.

Power and political power

It is perhaps clearer by now why I have kept a distance from those approaches that set 'power' at the heart of politics. Power can be a means, but in my view

---

10. For Stoppino, politics is not defined by power but by the 'search for power', action finalised towards power; Stoppino, *Potere e teoria politica*, chapter 8. Leaving aside my uneasiness with the concept of 'power' this conclusion overemphasises the search for public authority and somehow leaves out the search for final values connected with the search for public authority.

it cannot be either the nuclear element of political action or the source of a political good or warranty. Definition of that power which is political is difficult. Either power is always political (as it is for Lasswell, for example) or a definition of power that is political needs to resort to an underpinning locational principle (power that is political is that which emanates from certain loci). This last solution, however, is utterly unsatisfactory, as I have argued earlier (pp. 13–15): it makes a unified vision of political action impossible; it may exclude the political from anarchic and natural fields, and it leaves unsolved the issue of the political constitutions of the loci from which the political emanates. The request for compliance, in contrast, unifies all forms of political action. The differences among them emerge from the conditions of the different fields in which political action takes place. Requests for compliance are lightly political in anarchic fields, powerful but punctuated and unstable in natural fields and increasingly stabilised and generalised in authority and governmental fields.

My point is that there is a world of difference whether bindingness over others is applied via a direct utilisation of power/resources in dealings with other actors or whether compliance is stabilised over time and generalised to the entire membership of a system, *including those against which no 'power' has been used and no conflict has been waged*. To clarify the ambiguity that the concept of 'power' generates, let us discuss the simple but frequent example of the attribution of 'power' to a politically relevant actor – the Catholic Church, for example. The argument is that the 'power' of the Catholic Church depends on a skilful use of identity, cultural and symbolic resources.[11] This ideological power generates forms of compliance with the Church through the direct use of resources such as the expectation of salvation, confession and the remission of sins, the administration of sacraments and guidelines for redemption. However, this power is exercised over the membership group: Catholics, practising strong believers, ecclesiastics. It does not extend to non-believers, to those who do not care about salvation or to the fiercely anticlerical.

Extending *this* power outside the reference membership group, to non-members, is impossible. To obtain this extension, there must be a request for behavioural compliance that takes another form. Such a request will address the ruler rather than the non-members. It will therefore require resources different to the symbolic ones that work with the members. It needs resources that appeal to the ruler. This power is in principle independent of the power

---

11. Warren gives the example of the 'power' of the Church resting on identity, symbolic and cultural resources. Warren, M.E. (1999), 'What Is Political?', *Journal of Theoretical Politics*, 11: 207–31. The same problem exists in the infinite numbers of cases in which we read of the 'power' of employers, the power of trade unions or the power of any other group.

exercised over the Church's membership. In other words, it is a completely different 'power' that has only tenuous and uncertain connections with the other 'power', the ideological power over its specific membership.[12] Similarly, whatever 'power' an employer exerts over the workers in a firm applies only to them, not to all workers. An employer's power that applies to all workers needs other means to achieve it, other and different binding decisions and other backings. The concept of the power of any actor hides this crucial distinction and obfuscates these two different aspects. In other words, it confuses the distribution of 'endowments' within the authority field with the distribution of 'entitlements' in the governmental field.

Public goods

What type of good is the political warranty as it has been defined here? So far, we have used the terms 'public' and 'private' goods in a general sense, with the first referring to goods produced by the public authority and the second to goods produced by agreements between actors, deals or contracts. How does the political good fare in the light of the theoretical definitions of public and private goods in the theory of goods?[13] In this theory, private goods are both excludable and rivalrous. They are excludable because an individual can be excluded from consuming private goods unless she pays for them. They are rivalrous because whatever quantity of this type of good an individual consumes, no one else can consume. Public goods, on the contrary, are non-excludable because it is impossible to prevent those who have not paid for them from consuming them, and they are non-rivalrous because whatever an individual consumes of such a good does not limit consumption by others.

Is the 'political good', defined as the production of positive dispositions of all others to one's entitlements, excludable or non-excludable? If it is excludable, we can limit the consumption of the good to those who pay for it and

---

12. One may argue that the same power exercised over the membership group turns into a resource for support and pressure towards the ruler. However, this is an undue assumption. The power over the faithful rests on different resources to those necessary to affect the ruler (vote or mobilisation capacity, for instance). The idea of the 'power of the actor' confuses the two.

13. Samuelson, P. (1954), 'The Pure Theory of Public Expenditure', *Review of Economics and Statistics*, 36 (4): 387–89 develops this conceptualisation. Here, I leave aside other important developments of this theory. Buchanan adds 'club goods', where groups of individuals create private associations (clubs) to provide themselves with non-rivalrous but small-scale goods and services that they can enjoy while excluding non-members from participation and consumption of the benefits. Buchanan, James M. (1965), 'An Economic Theory of Clubs', *Economica*, 32 (125), N.S., pp. 1–14. Olstrom identifies 'common goods' or 'common pool resource goods', defined by their excludability (called 'subtractability') and also by non-rivalrousness (called 'difficulty of exclusion') referring to the exploitation of groundwater basins, lakes, irrigation systems, fisheries, forests and so on. Olstrom, E. (2005), *Understanding Institutional Diversity*, Princeton, NJ: Princeton University Press. Both club and common goods refer to the creation of what is here defined as an authority field, rather than a governmental field.

so contribute to providing it. A refusal to pay is in this case a refusal to grant your favourable disposition towards the entitlements of others. This usually generates the most radical sanctions on the part of the monopolistic producer of the warranty for the field. It is a direct attack on its core function, which, if numerically significant, endangers the nature of the governmental field itself and threatens to transform it into a natural field. Therefore, there are few ways, if any, not to pay. It is a compulsory exchange. You pay for the 'political good' with the forced, unavoidable and non-retrievable recognition of the rights to entitlements of others. You pay when you do not renounce, and you cannot renounce, your due share of compliance. This generalised disposition towards compliance with the entitlements of other actors is a cost that members of the field pay in exchange for a positive disposition towards their present and future entitlements.

In the accumulation of the legal order, no actor can separate what he accepts from what he rejects in order to limit or scale his own subjection within it. What the individual, either alone or in association, can do is to exchange his tolerance of what he dislikes (or does not care) for the mutual recognition of his own entitlements. In seeking his own quota of guaranteed compliance, the single actor must de facto recognise the quotas of others. Through this exchange, in a legalised form of government, constitutive predicaments remain unchallenged, the degree of fundamental opposition to the territorial group is reduced or the opposition is mitigated. Therefore, the political good apparently seems to be a private good for which you have to pay if you want to consume and for which there is no way to not pay or consume. In fact, the possibilities of not paying are very few and very costly.

At the same time, the cost of producing a positive attitude in others to your entitlements in the field is unaffected by the number of those who consume the political good. On the contrary, the more extended the group who consume it, the greater the production of it.[14] Production of the political good reproduces it rather than consuming it. Thus, the 'political good' looks like a public good because the cost of producing it is not fundamentally affected by the number of consumers.

The political good is the unintentional result of the interaction between the appetite of the political class for public authority and that of other actors for final values. The entire membership of the governmental field consumes it, and while they do so they also pay for it, as a positive disposition of the

---

14. In this sense, the 'political good' resembles a 'network good' in that current users gain when additional users consume it. Klemperer, Paul (2008, 2nd ed.), 'Network Goods (Theory)', in Steven N. Durlauf and Lawrence E. Blume (eds.), *The New Palgrave Dictionary of Economics*, London: Palgrave Macmillan; *The New Palgrave Dictionary of Economics Online*, Palgrave Macmillan, 21 June 2016, www.dictionaryofeconomics.com/article?id=pde2008_N000138. doi:10.1057/9780230226203.1176.

other members to one's own entitlements necessarily requires one to have a positive attitude to his entitlements. Therefore, the 'political good' seems non-rivalrous, like public goods, but you must pay in order to consume it, like private goods. This difficulty in characterising the political good in terms of the theory of goods evidences its nature as a 'meta-good'. The 'political' emerges and characterises itself when the logic of paying and consuming does not apply. Politics produces 'guaranteed rights', rights to any kind of goods: private, public, club or common pool resource goods. All these goods depend on a meta-good, which is the generalised and stabilised disposition of the other actors to recognise your guaranteed rights.

Social dilemmas

I have argued that collective action problems are not involved in the production of the political good. This thesis deserves a more extended discussion given the importance it has acquired in recent theorising about politics. In an institutional talk at the turn of the century, Elinor Olstrom argued that

> the theory of collective action is *the* central problem of political science. It is the core of the justification of the state. Collective action problems pervade international relations, face legislators when devising public budgets, permeate public bureaucracies, and are at the core of the explanation of voting, interest group formation, and citizens' control of government in a democracy.[15]

Social dilemmas and collective action problems have different names, including public good problems, shirking, free rider problems, moral hazard, credible commitment dilemmas, generalised social exchange, tragedy of the commons, exchanges of threats and so on. They all refer to an interaction context where interdependent individuals face choices for which the maximisation of short-term interest yields outcomes worse than feasible alternatives. There are assumptions about human behaviour, information and environmental conditions and individuals interact on these premises.[16] Any individual has the options of contributing or not contributing to a joint benefit. If everybody contributes, they achieve a net positive benefit. However, everybody

---

15. Olstrom, Elinor (1998), 'A Behavioural Approach to the Rational Choice Theory of Collective Action: Presidential Address, American Political Science Association', *The American Political Science Review*, 92: 1–22, p. 1.

16. The assumptions behind almost all models of social dilemmas are that (1) participants have common knowledge of the exogenously fixed structure of the situation and of the payoffs to be received by all individuals under a combination of strategies; (2) decisions about strategies are made independently, often simultaneously; (3) all participants have the same strategy available (in a symmetrical game); (4) no external actor (or central authority) is present to enforce agreements among participants about their choices; (5) individuals have mutually incompatible or jointly inconsistent interests (preferences), and not everybody can be simultaneously satisfied completely.

has the temptation to shift from the contributors to the non-contributors. The theoretical prediction is that everybody will do this and then the outcome will be a less valued payoff, which, however, is an equilibrium which no one has an interest in moving from. The situation is a dilemma because an outcome exists that would yield a better payoff for all the participants. This creates a conflict between individual and group rationality.[17]

It is unquestionably the case that these problems have attracted increasing attention from political scientists. I am not convinced, however, that collective action problems are the core problems of politics, at least as they are understood here. In my view, social dilemmas are likely to be frequently generated in anarchic and natural fields. As already discussed, they are a constitutive problem for the formation of authority fields. That is, they are a crucial aspect of any 'politics' seen as a system of action in which individual preferences are or must be aggregated through voluntary acts. They are at the core of those situations in which actors are free to join or leave social relationships and fields, to cooperate or not cooperate. In these circumstances, the problem is to explain the actors' capacity and/or willingness to cooperate in terms of their individual motivations and interests.

Problems of coordination inevitably emerge in any closed social field of confined actors. However, so does the natural tendency to search for and aim for the compliance of others as a precondition for the attainment of individual values. In governmental fields, confinement and monopolisation de facto introduce sanctions, which are not directly in the interest of those who compete for authority positions but are the unintended result of their interest in achieving, keeping and stabilising their ruling positions. Endangering or not defending the production of the political good would be fatal for these competing groups.

Therefore, when a new problem of cooperation emerges in a governmental field it will not be shaped as a problem of coordination among interdependent but autonomous individuals. Requests are not directed towards the other actors but they take the form of requests for stable and generalised compliance achieved by the ruler's production. The coordination that is so difficult to achieve in models of individualistic interactions is achieved by the ruler distributing and redistributing new entitlements, the compliance with which

---

17. I do not discuss these 'assumptions' in this book. See Green, Donald P. and Ian Schapiro (1994), *Pathologies of Rational Choice Theories. A Critique of Applications in Political Science*, New Haven, CT: Yale University Press. Nor do I intend to touch upon the question of whether politics should be seen as a mere problem of allocative efficiency irrespective of (1) endowments (rights, resources), which are seen as properly allocated; (2) preferences, outside the realm of technical treatment; (3) competence; and (4) integrity. On this topic, see March, James G. and Johan P. Olsen (1989), *Rediscovering Institutions. The Organizational Basis of Politics*, New York: The Free Press, p. 122.

of all the actors is guaranteed and stabilised if they do not want to endanger the stability of the binding order of the field from which all their other rights also depend on. Similarly, punishment is not an insurmountable obstacle to social dilemmas. If you deprive others of your positive disposition towards their guaranteed rights and violate the stabilised and generalised production of these guaranteed shares of mutual rights, you will be deprived of a proportional share of your own guaranteed rights by the guardian of the monopolistic provision of generalised and stabilised compliance.

This is how the monopolistic provision of behavioural compliance allows experimentation with solutions that are unthinkable in any other kind of field. Policy outcomes can be envisaged in which some actors have to accept losses so as not to further endanger their entitlements or in which the advantages gained by one set of actors (winners) are at least high enough to allow another set of actors (the losers) to be compensated. That is, only in governmental fields can the Kaldor optimality principle supersede the Pareto-optimality principle.[18] This is why politics can be a far superior principle for conflict resolution than all those based on voluntary agreements among individual actors.

It is doubtful whether ruler-subject relationships – which appear essential in most sophisticated forms of politics, as is difficult to empirically deny – can be framed with a social dilemma approach. Indeed, we can also identify social dilemmas in interactions among individuals and factions competing for public authority. However, it is interesting to note that when social dilemmas apply to interactions within the political class they usually privilege spheres of relative equality among actors – such as competing candidates, legislators, committee members and so on, that is, situations of low or weak monopolisation and confinement. I cannot qualify my argument more extensively due to the fact that in this book I am leaving out altogether a study of the internal institutional differentiation of rulership. We cannot forget, however, that exogenous authority, hierarchy, organisation, competence layering and impositions of outcomes fundamentally affect these interactions too.

How independent actors endowed with the possibility of unilateral action solve the problem of cooperation (in natural and anarchic fields) is not the core problem of politics. The core problem is the production of compliance, not the production of voluntarily achieved agreements. Spontaneous cooperation or non-cooperation by autonomous actors defines a tenuous form of the political.[19] To make social dilemmas the 'core' of political science pushes

---

18. Kaldor, N. (1939), 'Welfare Propositions of Economics and Inter-Personal Comparisons of Utility', *Economic Journal*, 49: 549–52.
19. On this point, see Warren, M. E. (1999), 'What Is Political?', *Journal of Theoretical Politics*, 11: 207–31.

into the corner the essential feature of the political – the production of compliance – and brings to the forefront its more tenuous and reassuring aspect – overcoming the inefficiency of coordination.

THE STRATIFICATION OF THE POLITICAL

Let me conclude by focusing on four features of the political that are often implicitly muted or poorly underscored: the *stratification, expansion/contraction, autonomy* and *ultimacy* of the political.

In the customary sense in which we use the term 'politics', we indicate a pluri-dimensional process: politics as

(a) the process through which ordinary citizens unite their wills in the form of authority fields and constitute politically relevant actors (*the politics of participation and collective action*);
(b) the process in which authority fields as politically relevant actors exchange support resources with factions of the elite competing for authority positions (*the politics of support and pressure*); and
(c) the process in which these factions struggle among themselves for public authority (*the politics of competition*).

The 'policy process' that attracts so much attention in contemporary political research is not mentioned here as a fourth dimension of the conventional political process. This is because from the point of view outlined here 'policies' are merely the goals of the first two processes and the means of the third. From the political point of view, concrete policies are important because of their instrumental roles as goals and tools in the three processes mentioned.

This view leads us to a key feature of authority and governmental fields: their *stratification* in relation to rule. This sounds like a trivial and uncontroversial property of the political, and so it was for classical political science. However, this primordial aspect of the political is the one that is most systematically overlooked in contemporary political analysis, which often prefers to work with flattened landscapes peopled by generic actors such as citizens, consumers, taxpayers, voters, representatives and so forth or with simplified dyadic relations such as voters/representatives, taxpayers/governments or consumers/firms.

In governmental fields, there is a differentiation between the search for public authority and the search for and defence of specific goods and values. The struggle for positions of public authority separates from the competition for 'allocation of values'. Political action forks into the use of resources to acquire the role of a monopolistic provider, on the one hand, and the search for entitlement eligibility, on the other hand. The dominant form of exchange takes place between those who aim for public authority – individuals and groups that are *directly involved in the struggle for public authority*, let us call them the *political class*[20] – and those who aim for specific entitlements as guaranteed rights. Politics thus acquires the familiar double logic of political entrepreneurs competing for political authority and politically relevant actors and ordinary citizens searching for 'entitlements'. In other words, the layering neatly corresponds to the differentiation of final values: support/opposition in competition for public authority versus concrete final goods and values.

Next to the political class, therefore, lies a group more difficult to define, which we can label *politically relevant actors*. These can be clearly differentiated from the political class by the fact that they *do not* aim to enter the direct fight for public authority. These actors are 'politically relevant' because they control and master supra-individual resources that can be brought to bear on the competition for authority among factions of the political class in the form of support and opposition. Politically relevant actors are all those individual, collective, corporate or institutional actors[21] such as interest group leaders, businesspersons and associations; NGO and social movement representatives; professional associations; public intellectuals and leading media figures and owners and so on. Their higher stakes foster their capacity to create and constitute authority fields and to engage in instrumental and strategic political action.

Politically relevant actors are less clearly distinguishable from the third layer, which is constituted by *ordinary citizens*, who own only individual resources, are normally not organised, have limited political competence, are poorly informed and are only occasionally or intermittently involved in political matters.[22] The resources ordinary citizens can bring to bear on the various

---

20. Gaetano Mosca coined this expression in Mosca, Gaetano (1896; revised 1923), *Elementi di scienza politica*, Torino: Fratelli Bocca Editori. The book appeared in English in 1939 under the title *The Ruling Class*, New York and London: McGraw Hill Book Company, Inc. Mosca attributes a wider meaning to 'political class' than the one I use here: the set of hierarchies that morally and materially rule a society. I use this expression because it is less ambiguous than other terms such as 'ruling elites', 'power elites', 'dominant elites' or 'political elites' in identifying the stratum of actors directly aiming and competing for public authority positions. For me, it identifies an empirical set of actors, and I thereby avoid entering the intricacies and debates of elite theory. For this, see the critical review by Dahl, R. (1958), 'A Critique of the Ruling Elite Model', *The American Political Science Review*, 52: 463–69.

21. This book does not discuss the distinction between individual, collective, corporate and institutional actors. For a sensitive treatment – which, however, excludes institutional actors – see Scharpf, *Games Real Actors Play*, pp. 56–60.

22. The abyssal average differences in information between different sections of the population was originally pointed out in Lazarsfeld, P. F., B. Berelson and H. Gaudet (1944), The *People's Choice: How the Voter Makes Up His Mind in a Presidential Campaign*, New York: Columbia University Press; systematised in Converse, P. (1964), 'The Nature of Belief Systems in Mass Publics', in D. E. Apter (ed.), *Ideology and Discontent*, New York: The Free Press of Glencoe, pp. 206–61; and has since then been confirmed by overwhelming evidence on many countries and periods.

factions in the political class depend on their occasional capacity to make numbers count in the latter's concern about accession to rulership. In mob politics, civil disorders, street demonstrations, civic disobedience, elections and referenda, mobilisation conveys relatively little specific information to the politics of pressure.[23] The vagueness of these requests for compliance may nevertheless be compensated for by their number, and they can be decisive for factional strife within the political class, that is, in the politics of competition. In the majority of these cases, however, ordinary citizens are usually mobilised by politically relevant actors and only more rarely self-activate as true collective actors.

These three groups are hierarchically layered with respect to the political element of the production of behavioural compliance. The porosity of the boundaries between them may generate some uncertainty of attribution. Notwithstanding this, it is surprising that the current debate in political science often almost entirely overlooks this stratification principle with respect to public authority. Whether one accepts the layering proposed here of 'political class', 'politically relevant actors' and 'ordinary citizens' or prefers a different one, the fact should not be forgotten or overlooked that politics *is stratified* in terms of distance from command in any context and at any level. It is mystifying to present the political as a flattened landscape of coequals, autonomous and independent actors characterised only by unilateral options in conjunction with external constraints. It is my contention – further elaborated in the following sections – that a great deal of the constructions of states of nature, game theoretical models and social dilemma situations derive from and are built on an ignorance of political stratification. This 'flattening view', as I shall call it, proves utterly artificial in most political relations, although it may adequately model other social relationships. It derives from situations where stratification elements are tenuous (demand/supply, consumers/producers, etc.), and it is unreflectively extended to more heavily stratified relationships.

THE EXPANSION/CONTRACTION OF THE POLITICAL

In governmental fields, 'politics' has a potential, and in many ways, intrinsic, expansionary logic. In order to generate compliance and to sustain political production via the distribution of guaranteed rights, it is necessary to control

---

23. This is one of the main points in the seminal work by Verba, Nie and Kim on the tradeoff between information content and capacity to exert pressure through different forms of political action. Verba, Sidney, Norman H. Nie and Jae-on Kim (1978), *Participation and Political Equality. A Seven Nation Comparison*, London: Cambridge University Press.

additional resources by locking actors in. It is necessary to prevent or limit the exit options of those actors or resources over which these rights have to be exercised. Hence, in governmental fields there is a tendency to limit the exit options of actors, resources and territories, leading to an ever-growing accumulation of guaranteed compliance in order to guarantee rights. This is the source of the frightening but consistent Hobbesian argument that only a total tyranny can distribute and preserve order and stabilise governmental fields. However, there are counterforces too. Actors also want to be de-confined, and factions of the political class may sustain these claims.

Within governmental fields, there is always a combination of anarchic, natural and authority fields. Therefore, there are continual attempts to transform social relationships and fields from one type to another, continual attempts to unlock people and resources by actors who expect improvements in their life chances if they achieve this and continual attempts to transform natural and authority fields into governmental fields by actors who expect improvements in their own 'rights' from this change. De-confinement is a continual crucial process at the core of political production. In fact, we could say that the political process is characterised by actors continually fighting to confine and to de-confine other actors with the aim of achieving command or limiting the process of competing instigations.

As different fields offer different opportunities for the utilisation of resources, actors have preferences about which type of field is best for their interactions with other actors. Their instigations may seek to keep an issue out of the selection procedure for command and reserve it for anarchic or natural fields, where they expect to have more resources and chances of obtaining a favourable outcome in the absence of command. Contrariwise, the selection of a single command is actively aimed at whenever individual and personal resources are insufficient to force exchanges or to obtain acquisitions through direct political actions directed at other actors. To these ends, individual actors aim to multiply their instigation capacity by cooperating with other similarly intentioned individuals in the constitution of authority fields whose aim is to keep alive and persistently pursue the intents of the promoters, winning over other people and generating positive orientations among at least a part of the public. To promote or deter a command, actors seek to keep their requests alive even if a different command is issued. Confinement, like de-confinement, is never fully achieved or guaranteed. When the permanent withdrawal of crucial resources is a credible threat, the governmental features of the arena tend to dilute into a less governmental environment in which the rationality of key actors aims at the best allocation and use of their resources. In this situation, the credibility of the commitment to produce generalised and stabilised compliance falls in parallel with its scope and reach. What exiters no longer need is no longer guaranteed for the non-exiters.

Under different historical circumstances, with a prevalence of confinement/de-confinement requests, politics *pulses*, in the sense that it tends to expand and contract the production of guaranteed rights. This pulsing also relates to the continual shifting between phases of prevalence of private interests and phases of public action.[24] In other words, the political scientist needs to analyse the entire political process with special attention to the constant dynamics of commands versus competing instigations, the corresponding confinement/de-confinement of actors and transformations of one type of field into another. This is the *political meaning* and what is crucially at stake in the midst of the infinite number of goods, decisions and policies constantly produced and redefined by the political process.

What is uniquely demoniac about politics is that its components – the confinement of actors, the search for compliance, the intrinsic predicaments in the constitution of a governmental field, the competition for political authority and the production of entitlements – are interchangeable, and one can convert into another. Each component can be a means and an end in itself, with no exogenous rule to discipline the best combination. Various forms of confinement are means to political authority as much as political authority can be an instrument of confinement in its search to feed itself. A reduction of exit options functional to the production and distribution of entitlements can easily transform into an end in itself. The search for behavioural compliance can be a means to sustain political authority, with the competition for this authority degenerating into a run towards an irresponsible distribution of entitlements.

THE AUTONOMY OF THE POLITICAL

Governmental (and authority) fields also generate a specific configuration of the 'autonomy of the political' which cannot emerge in the other types of field. Despite often being thought of as a misread concept, the 'autonomy of the political' is a fundamental factor, unawareness of which is the sign of any non- or a-political thinking. The concept is misunderstood whenever it is used to indicate the autonomy of the political from other resources (ideational, economic, legal, etc.). Other resource holders do indeed sanction, influence, condition and persuade, and it is hardly thinkable that the political class is insulated from this politics of pressure. The autonomy of the political acquires sense with reference to the aforementioned political stratification

---

24. As discussed in Hirschman, Albert O. (1982), *Shifting Involvements: Private Interests and Public Action*, Princeton, NJ: Princeton University Press.

of the governmental field. The division between the struggle/competition[25] for positions of public authority and the struggle/competition for substantive decisions that distribute entitlements corresponds to the division between the struggle for *who* will occupy political positions and the struggle for *what* is or will be done using these positions. The political manifests its autonomy in the struggle for 'who', but it is inappropriate to use this expression with reference to the struggle for 'what'. In the latter struggle, actors will always use resources distributed unevenly to achieve their preferred final values. Although in specific circumstances this second form of autonomy may materialise,[26] my claim is that the political is *always* autonomous in the first sense.

The autonomy of the struggle for public authority manifests itself in three distinct elements. The first element of autonomy is what I call the 'mutual instrumentality' of the two struggles referred to earlier. The web of binding decisions and the multilateral system of recognition of entitlements are eventual unintended consequences of these interactions. The prevailing policies of protection, jurisdiction regulation, arbitration or allocation in various domains, which appear as the essence or the function of the political process, are in fact only a function of the search for public authority among competing groups in the political class. Similarly, the support/opposition that relevant political actors and ordinary citizens direct to competing sections of the political class is only a function of their appetite and desire for final values. In this mutual instrumentality (politicians instrumentalise supporters for their ends, and supporters instrumentalise politicians for theirs), politics acquires a great deal of independence from other realms of activity. Politics depends on a fundamental falsehood of ends which are mutually sustaining.

Second, victory in the struggle for public authority is an indispensable condition for the implementation of specific political proposals and programmes, for the distribution of concrete final values in the form of entitlements. That is, in the struggle for public authority 'what has to be achieved' is subordinated to achievement of the positions to deliver it. Engagement and

---

25. 'Struggle' implies no or very few rules of the game; 'competition' is usually regulated. There can only be competition for public authority if stable institutions define the rules of the game.

26. Marx and Engels suggest that in certain circumstances – when the antagonist classes balance each other – political production acquires a degree of independence from socio-structural conditioning. A similar case is that of the type of regime that Linz and Chahabi label 'sultanistic'. Totalitarianism is a third obvious instance. See Engels, F. (1884; 1942), *The Origin of the Family, Private Property, and the State*, New York: International Publishers, pp. 290–91; Marx, K. (1852; 1963), *The 18 Brumaire of Louis Bonaparte*, New York: International Publishers; Chebabi, Houchang E. and Juan J. Linz (eds.) (1998), *Sultanistic Regimes*, Baltimore: Johns Hopkins University Press, pp. 3–25; Neuman, Franz (1957), *Notes on the Theory of Dictatorship, in the Democratic and the Authoritarian State*, Glencoe: The Free Press, pp. 233–56; and Linz, Juan (2000), *Totalitarian and Authoritarian Regimes. With a Major New Introduction*, London: Lynne Rienner.

then victory in the 'struggle for who' is a necessary and unescapable condition for implementing any 'programme'. Only effectiveness determines and standardises the praxis to this end. Individuals, groups or intellectuals may elaborate ideas, programmes and doctrines, but they cannot aspire to the role of political actor if they are unwilling to enter the struggle for public authority. They can only limit their action to persuasion or playing the role of the unarmed prophet that Machiavelli attributed to the meteoric rise and fall of Savonarola in fifteenth-century Florence.

Following on from the previous point, the fight for public authority is largely independent of substantive proposals, that is, of the 'what' is or will be delivered as final values. The struggle for public authority has the praxeological characteristic of being composed of a number of rules of the game, tactics and stratagems that are basically the same in all the political groups that effectively fight for public authority. The rules that teach how to win are at the margins, if not beyond, of the rules of correct competition, of how to play fairly.[27] Qualities usually perceived as positive – honesty, reliability and so on – are in principle as good as qualities usually perceived as negative, such as falsehood, exploitation of the weaknesses of adversaries – including personal ones – obstructionism, filibustering and so on. Their autonomy lies in the forms, tactics and stratagems in the struggle for authority that all the actors have to put into practice in the fight to reach such positions, and independently of the content they will eventually give to their ruling. In passing, note that in the competition for 'who', instigations can be issued that it is difficult to define as prohibited, and so it is difficult for the instigator to be found guilty in legal terms. In other words, in the competition for political authority, instigations and requests for compliance are 'innocent' in legal terms and are rarely legally pursued. While, in principle, certain 'actions' can be traced to the person who has suggested or inspired them, and his advisors can be counted as accomplices or mandators, this is rarely possible for the political instigations that pertain to tactics in the competition for authority.[28]

Whatever the final programmatic content, be it that of the executive committee of the bourgeoisie or of the proletariat, the means to exercise it pass

---

27. The best source on the tension between morality and effectiveness is without doubt the extended literature in the Christian Church on the subject of casuistry. As this is daunting reading, we can consult Bayley, one of the very few authors who have focused attention on these varying praxes, establishing a distinction between 'rules of the game' and 'pragmatic rules' in political competition (Bayley, Frederick J. (1970), *Stratagems and Spoils. A Social Anthropology of Politics*, Oxford: Basil Blackwell), and the twelve tales on the political art of exploiting agendas and rules in Riker, William H. (1986), *The Art of Political Manipulation*, New Haven, CT: Yale University Press. This latter is more about the political art of reframing alternatives in such a way that people will be forced to join without their preference being satisfied.

28. While, of course, the followers performing the instigated actions are held responsible and found guilty.

through the means to achieve it. The means to achieve it are largely independent, and therefore in this sense autonomous, of the programme and concrete decisions eventually enforced. Irrespective of the sometimes very large differences in their ideological and political goals, the different factions in the political class struggling for authority are similar if we focus on the means, tactics and resources they resort to in the attempt to win the struggle.

The last component of the autonomy of the political is that in the fight for public authority there is no 'substantive' specific or sectorial competence that can help. Only competences which are inherently 'political' – in the sense of pertaining to specific tactics and stratagems for the use of resources for acquiring positions and roles – will be relevant and useful. In the fight for public authority, substantive competences may be of no use, which is the eternal misunderstanding of any technocratic claim or approach. Specifically political competencies are more general and pertain to the capacity to combine different interests, to mobilise support and specific resources, to successfully use tactics and stratagems to obtain advantages and to generate damage to adversaries, or to discredit or blame the adversary in the eyes of relevant powers or the common citizens.

These three elements are the constitutive aspects of what defines the 'autonomy of the political', an expression that has no meaning in any other sense.

THE ULTIMACY OF THE POLITICAL

Governmental fields – and in this case only governmental fields – can finally be characterised by their 'ultimacy'.[29] This ultimacy depends on the fact that the monopolistic provider of compliance remains the arbiter of the means by which non-governmental fields are formed, protected, enabled, displaced or overshadowed. It retains the ultimate capacity to decide, which is what most observers identify as the frightening or evil aspect of politics and political institutions. This does not mean that all decisions are collectivised and brought under the direct control of the monopolistic ruler. Quite the contrary, we historically observe and may theoretically imagine quite a high level of decisional autonomy being left to other types of field within the governmental one. This means that *ultimately*, and particularly in those cases in which the territorial group is challenged by contradictory instigations, the existence of

---

29. Poggi uses this term with reference to the state; Poggi, G. (1990), *The State: Its Nature, Development and Prospects*, Stanford, CA: Stanford University Press. I use it with reference to the production of stabilised and generalised compliance in governmental fields.

one effective monopolistic provider of compliance may lead to a withdrawing of all the delegations thanks to which other fields operate.

The monopolistic provider enforces the parameters of interaction in the economic sphere in such a way as to enable individuals, firms and other economic actors to deploy their economic potential. The monopolistic provider 'sets and enforces rules of conduct (e.g., contract law) and limits to market interactions (e.g., outlawing trading in slaves or buying public offices, or legislating for conditions of labour and environmental standards)'.[30] This monopolistic provider also enables the associational relations of civil society. Voluntary associations may solve collective problems to the extent that the monopolistic provider enables them to do so and protects them from alternative solutions.

The logical and empirical possibility of hybrid cases that combine characteristics of different fields also confirms the ultimacy of governmental fields. As mentioned, fields are not mutually exclusive and there are hybrid cases in which different fields can be 'nested' within one another. In an authority field there are obviously interactions among members who are anarchic or natural, but they must be interaction patterns that are not typical of the authority field, which would otherwise dissolve. Actors in natural fields are confined, a condition incompatible with the freedom of exit that characterises authority or anarchic fields. In contrast, a governmental field is compatible with a set of subfields in which interactions can be anarchic, natural and authority-based. Hybrid combinations do not necessarily endanger the field. The authority in the governmental field can opt to define and protect anarchic fields, for example, to protect the rights of buyers and sellers in the market. The governmental field can host situations of asymmetry of resources, such as when defining minimal conditions for political competition and leaving actors free to use whatever resources they can muster in the competition. A governmental field can cultivate and license authority fields with associational or functional autonomy. Membership groups can de facto exist within and against a governmental field. In other words, hybridisation of the governmental field with other types of fields is always possible and, as argued in the previous section 'The autonomy of the political' the dynamics of this hybridisation should be the core concern of the political analyst.

In certain historical-geographical circumstances, we observe that spheres and sets of relationships enjoy considerable autonomy and independence from external influences. Nevertheless, we need to distinguish whether they enjoy this because they exclude the ultimate existence of a monopolistic provider or simply because they have acquired or conquered this degree

---

30. Warren, M.E. (1999), 'What Is Political?', *Journal of Theoretical Politics*, 11: 207–31, esp. p. 228.

of autonomy while operating within the range permitted by a monopolistic provider. Even if the level of autonomy and unilateral action of actors we observe is very high and we deem it unthinkable for such autonomy to be withdrawn or reduced, this possibly always exists in different historical circumstances, and particularly whenever the stability and survival of the territorial group is at stake. Similarly, of course, the possibility always exists that during such challenges the competition between alternative claimants for the monopoly of compliance production destroys governmental fields and turns them into natural fields.

In anarchic and natural fields, people may cooperate and self-organise. They can voluntarily generate an internal provider of compliance, transforming their relationships into an authority field. They can self-organise differently without the establishment of a formal association.[31] People confined by the utilisation of a common resource can design institutional rules and perhaps functional authorities to regulate such special use, avoiding the anarchic solution represented by the privatisation and marketisation of quotas of the resource or the governmental solution of public regulation of the same use. The 'common pool resource' literature focuses on this subset of self-organisation in natural fields: institutions designed by users when the conditions for confining refer to a common use of a resource, a special type of confinement.[32]

Groups of people such as stakeholders in a natural field of this type may communicate, exchange and cooperate on a continual basis and set up rules to stabilise these arrangements, rules that regulate the use of a specific good. However, they cannot generalise such compliance production beyond the limits of their membership group; they cannot transform the shares of endowments reciprocally agreed into guaranteed rights that enjoy the protection typical of a governmental field. If these endowments are not transformed into 'guaranteed rights', with which every other possible actor's disposition to comply is guaranteed, it is unclear, for example, what happens if new claimants intrude in the governing of the commons as agreed by the original group.

This suggests that development of these normative orders is possible only in the shadow of a governmental field that guarantees at least non-interference by other potential claimants and, if it happens, punishment for their intrusion.

---

31. The origin of the idea of institutions as spontaneous and self-enforcing orders resulting from an evolutionary approach can be found in Hayek, F. (1973), *Law, Legislation and Liberty: Rules and Orders*, vol. 1, Chicago: University of Chicago Press. For a review of the endogenous generation of institutions, see Aoki, Masahiko (2000), 'Institutional Evolution as Punctuated Equilibria', in C. Ménard (ed.), *Institutions, Contracts and Organizations*, Cheltenham, UK: Edward Elgar, pp. 11–33.

32. See the classic study by Hardin, Garrett (1968), 'The Tragedy of the Commons', *Science, NS*, 162: 1243–48. An excellent comprehensive summary of the literature on 'governing the commons' is Olstrom, Elinor (2010), 'Beyond Markets and States: Polycentric Governance and Complex Economic Systems', *American Economic Review*, 100: 1–33.

The cooperation that is achieved is achieved because of this protection, not instead of it or as an alternative to it. 'Governing of the commons' solutions are examples of the conditions under which individuals may develop normative standards among themselves and orders of their own without exogenous intervention. These are not conditions alternative to the governmental field, but one of the forms of delegation of spheres of autonomy that are valid only under the assumption of the ultimacy of governmental field compliance production.

This literature, perhaps, overgeneralises its result. Next to these forms of spontaneous and polycentric cooperation there remain by far more numerous cases in which actors collectively organise not for self-management but to create and transform institutional arrangements through political means by seeking regulation of the field through the production of stabilised and generalised behavioural compliance by the monopolistic provider.[33] A specification of the conditions under which individuals confined by the use of a common pool resource may effectively self-organise and cooperate is an important result, but interpretation of this result as a solution *alternative* to that provided by the market or by authority (both depending on the political warranty) is overstretched.

It is an optical illusion to derive the nature of the monopolistic provider of compliance (or of the state) from fields that produce no compliance or only unstable and limited forms of compliance. While it seems impossible – both historically and theoretically – to derive the forms of *monopolistic* provision of compliance from synallagmatic relations among autonomous actors, it is possible – both logically and historically – to identify the conditions under which the monopolistic provider guarantees spheres of synallagmatic relations, functional authority and natural competition.

Economic transactions hang on rules that defend the rights based on which exchanges can be entertained. The legal system hangs on politics as far as the production and modification of those rights are concerned. What does politics hang on? Curiously, the usual answer is that politics 'hangs' on the rule of law and on fundamental (often economic) rights. That is, it hangs on those same basic elements that it upholds. In the most auspicious experiences we observe rights and the rule of law being firmly established, and we perceive the political process to be channelled and disciplined by legal rules and respect for rights. This is indeed the situation in stabilised, pacified, legalised

---

33. Particularly in the history of labour unions and their struggle to reach institutional recognition, to obtain collective rights to negotiate and contract, to block and resist legal action against them. In the special case of fishermen, Holm describes the emergence of a system of rules that bind them together united against fish merchants and the way the fishermen manage to institutionalise these rules into law. Holm, P. (1995), 'The Dynamics of Institutionalisation: Transformation Processes in Norwegian Fisheries', *Administrative Science Quarterly*, 40: 398–422.

situations, that is, in all those circumstances in which the political, having produced its most benign effects, broadly denies and limits itself. In these cases, the political disciplines itself to a surprising degree, and it is reconciled with those same external normative constraints that it ultimately grounds. This generates the hazardous optical illusion of the political depending on or deriving from the individual interactions that the normative framework allows. These normative constraints, nevertheless, reveal their unstable and eventually ephemeral nature in different and special circumstances in which widespread non-compliance ultimately challenges and offends the orderly political production of guaranteed rights.

The political cannot hang on to anything other than itself, and when necessary it is forced to pull itself out of the swamp by its own pigtails, like Baron von Muenchhausen.

Afterword

Much as a little book like this did not require an extended introduction, it is in no need of a summary conclusion. This concluding note only underlines once again that as a result of simplifying assumptions I have left three fundamental issues in the dark. I have spoken of 'actors' while overlooking the complexities involved in defining nuclear human actors and the even greater complexity of the constitution of supra-individual actors – aggregate, collective, corporate and institutional ones. I have assumed unified 'rulers' and 'rulership' while overlooking the complex institutional differentiation of the authority and governmental fields. I have mentioned the ideal-type structures of interactions among actors – negotiation, competition, cooperation and conflict – without elaborating on the recurrent patterns of behaviour (non-institutional, prescribed) that substantiate them. In short, I have left out 'political actors', 'political institutions' and 'political structures'. There are a few scant references here and there to these aspects in the text, but they are occasional, incomplete and unsystematic, to say the least.

I have focused on a theoretical elaboration of nuclear political action and nuclear politics, and perhaps this can be a justification for these limitations. However, I entertain the idea that a nuclear theory of political action and the political must be, and can be, the theoretical foundation on which understanding of political actors, institutions and structures should rest. This is a big claim, a big challenge and a different job. In the end, however, nuclear political action theory will be justified only if it helps in facing the challenge.

Index

Note: Page references for a table are italicized.

abuse of command, 87
accumulation of enforcement resources, 74–82; alliances and, 74; collective action, 74, 78–79; domestic exchanges, 86; English Glorious Revolution, 85–86; extension of the area of command, 83–84; external threats, 84–86; limitations on, 82–87; NIE literature on, 75; rationalistic perspective, 75; theoretical literature on, 75; third-parties and, 75–78, 80
acquiescence, 39. *See also* compliance
acquisitions, 111–13; political warranty and, 121; synallagmatic relationship, 120–21
activities, politics as, 11–13
agenda setting, power as, 47
aggregation: interaction among actors, 38n24; politics as, 21–24
allocations, 102; authoritative, 20, 118; politics as, 19–21
anarchic fields, 92–94; actors in, 93; compliance and final values, 109–15, *114*; international relations theory, 93–94; transitions, 108–9

anticipated reactions, 57–58
appraisal respect, 33n14
Aquinas, St. Thomas, 5, 7
arbitration, 102, 118
Arendt, H., 10
Aristotle, 2, 4–5, 23
Augustine, St., 7
authoritativeness, 120, 124
authority, in governmental fields, 140. *See also* public authority
authority fields, 94–100; actors in, 94; alternative providers, 97; collective action and, 97–98; command mechanisms, 96–97; compliance and final values, 109–15, *114*; compliance production, 96; constitution, 99; irregular pyramid, 98; legal order, 96; as multipliers of individual capacities, 95–96; political entrepreneurs and, 96; trade unions and political parties as, 99–100; transitions, 108–9
autonomy: of political, 7, 136–39; of society, 8–9; of struggle for public authority, 137–39; of subsystems, 86n46

behavioural compliance. *See* compliance
Bible, 41
bilateral agreements, 69
boundaries, 64–72; coincidence of, 67, 68; concept of, 65; confinement of actors, 68–72; degree of importance, 68n15; effectiveness of, 67; locking-in mechanisms, 65; nature of, 66–67; permeability of, 67; type of, 67
Brunner, Otto, 82–83
business organizations, 95

cabinets, 107, 108
Catholic Church, 126
Catlin, George E. G., 17
Christianity, 5
circumscription of actors, 70. *See also* confinement of actors
citizenship, 4
civil society: autonomy of, 8–9; state *vs.*, 8
civitas, 5
closed fields, 68–69; compliance production in, 69–70; interactions in, 71. *See also* boundaries
code-based behaviour, 43
coercion, and power, 16–19
coercive circumscription, 70
collective action enforcement, 74, 78–79
collective facility, power as, 46
collective good, 79
Collingwood, R. G., 10
command: abuse of, 87; ambition for, 42; lust for, 41–42; monopolisation of, 72–89; satisfaction of, 40–41
common pool resource, 141
competencies, 139
compliance: acquisition by others, 44; anticipated reactions, 57–58; as desired good, 41; explicit requests for, 54; fields of political action and, 109–15, *114*; formalisation, 88–89; honour and, 43; manipulation, 56–57;

monopolisation of, 72–89; moral-motivated action and, 44; non-explicit requests for, 54; persuasion, 56; power and, 46–50; psychologists on, 39; sanctions, 54–55. *See also* governmental fields
Comte, A., 9
conditioning, 56
confinement of actors, 61–72, 135; coercive circumscription, 70; compliance production, 71–72; environmental circumscription, 70; exit, 62–65, 70; interactions, 71; original confinement, 70; population pressure circumscription, 70; resource concentration, 70. *See also* boundaries
conflict: inequality of exit, 64; politics as, 15–16
conformity, 39
constitution, 4; defined, 106n22
constitutionalisation of rights, 124
contracts, 119–20; enforced by third parties, 76; market transactions, 75; political warranty, 121; property rights, 121
contractual relations, 118
Cranston, Maurice, 12
cultural hegemony, power as, 46

Dahl, Robert A., 29
de Cervantes, Miguel, 30
decisional capacity, power as, 47
de-confinements, 71; as core of political production, 135; elements of, 70
deep ecology school, 13
de Jouvenel, Bertrand, 10, 18, 19, 24n64, 38, 50–52, 53, 59, 103
democracy, 3, 7
denuded politics, 10, 10n19, 11
depersonalisation, 88–89
dictatorship, theory of, 86
directiveness, 38
dismembered politics, 11–24. *See also* politics
Dunn, John, 10

Easton, David, 20
Eckstein, H., 19
economic growth, 27–28
economic production process, 120
economic rights, 124
economic transactions, 142
employers' power, 127
endowments, 113–14, 117, 141
enforcement resources, accumulation of, 74–82; alliances and, 74; collective action, 74, 78–79; domestic exchanges, 86; English Glorious Revolution, 85–86; extension of the area of command, 83–84; external threats, 84–86; limitations, 82–87; NIE literature on, 75; rationalistic perspective, 75; ruler/subject relationship, 82–87; theoretical literature on, 75; third-parties and, 75–78, 80
English Glorious Revolution, 85–86
entitlements, 113–14, 120, 127–29, 133, 136; as conferred powers, 123; as guaranteed powers, 122; idea and concept of, 123–24; multilateral guaranteed compliances, 124; public authority, 125; things included in, 122
environmental circumscription, 70
ethics and politics, 5
exit, 62–65, 70; barriers to, 64; boundary building, 64–65 (*see also* boundaries); Hirschman's concept, 62–64; as impersonal, 62; individual costs of, 64; inequality of, 64; state and options of, 63; voice and, 62–63. *See also* confinement of actors
expansion/contraction, 134–36
explicit requests for compliance, 54
external threats, 84–86

false consciousness, power as, 47
fields of political action, 91–115; final values, types of, 109–15, *114*; request for compliance, types of, 109–15, *114*; transitions, 106–9; types, 91–106
Finer, S. E., 85
formalisation, 88–89
Foucault, Michel, 46
Frohock, F. M., 13n29, 38, 38n25

Gibbon, Edward, 41
goods: collective, 79; political, 127–29; private, 127; public goods, 120, 127–29. *See also* values
government, 3
governmental fields, 102–6; authority in, 140; autonomy, 136–39; compliance and final values, 109–15, *114*; compliance production, 102, 103; confinement of actors, 102, 105; constitution, 103, 104; defined, 102; expansion/contraction, 134–36; human group constituted as, 103; human interactions, 106; legitimacy predicament, 103–4; membership predicament, 103; political process in, 118; predicaments, 103–5; production function, 118; rule predicament, 103; stratification, 132–34; transitions, 107–9; ultimacy, 139–43
Gramsci, Antonio, 46
Greek conception of politics, 2–6
guaranteed rights, 129; expansion/contraction, 134–36
gubernaculum, 82

Hammond, Thomas, 81
Hart, H. L. A., 123
Hegel, G. W. F., 8
hierarchy: market failure and, 118
Hintze, O., 85
Hirschman, A. O., 62–64
Hobbes, Thomas, 6, 7, 8, 81n34, 86
honour, 33–37; compliance and, 43; loss of, 34; right to respect, 34, 35; sociology, 34; violation of legal rules and moral norms, 34

horizontal conception of politics, 2–7.
  See also vertical conception of
  politics
human rights, 124
Hume, David, 119

ideology, power as, 47
imperium, 82
instigations, 50–58; anticipated
  reactions, 57–58; conditioning, 56;
  intentional, 49; manipulation, 56–57;
  persuasion, 56; sanctions, 54–55
institutional locus, politics as, 13–15
interactions: among locked-in actors,
  71; mode of, 68
interest, 30–32, 35–37; non-contextual,
  32; non-relational, 32; self-interest
  vs., 36n19
interest-based behaviours, 45
internal peace monopolisation, 83
international borders, 66
international relations theory, 93–94
isonomia, 3

jurisdictio, 82
jurisdiction, 102, 118
juris societas, 5

Kaldor optimality principle, 131
Kaplan, A., 40, 68n18

Lasswell, Harold, 17, 18–19, 29, 38, 40,
  42, 46, 50, 52, 68n18, 91n1
law and politics, 9, 88–89, 106, 124
law of conservative exclusion, 51, 53,
  73n24
legal adjudication, 124
legal discourse of formalisation, 88–89
legal system, 124, 142
loss of honour, 34
Luhmann, Niklas, 46
Lukes, Steven, 47

Machiavelli, N., 6, 7, 138
man: non-political, 2; as political
  animal, 2

manipulation, 56–57
market failure: emergence of hierarchy
  from, 118; production of public
  goods, 124
market transactions, contracts and, 75
Marxist conception of power, 46
Maslowian hierarchy of needs and
  desires, 41
Meinecke, Friedrich, 41–42
Merriman, Charles E., 29
Miller, Gary, 81
mode of interaction, 68
monopolisation: of command, 72–89;
  compliance and, 72–89; defined, 72;
  internal peace, 83; limitations on,
  82–87; sovereignty, 82–83
Montague, Edward Wortley, 41
moral activist, 43
moral-based behaviours, 45
morality, 32–33, 35–37, 45; compliance
  and, 44; right to respect, 35
motivation for action, 29–37; Bible and,
  41; honour, 33–37; interest, 30–32,
  35–37; morality, 32–33, 35–37;
  political, 44
Mouffe, Chantal, 15
multilateral agreements, 69
multilateral guaranteed compliances, 124
multiparty coalition cabinet, 107
mutual instrumentality, 137

Nash equilibrium, 22
natural fields, 100–102; actors
  in, 100–101, 140; compliance
  and final values, 109–15, *114*;
  compliance in, 101–2; self-
  organisation in, 141; stakeholders
  in, 141; transitions, 108
negotiated agreements. *See* contractual
  relations
neighbour predation, 86
new institutional economics (NIE)
  literature, 75
non-confinement of actors, 69
non-explicit requests for
  compliance, 54

non-political man, 2
nuclear political action, 29–60

Oakeshott, M., 10, 12
obedience, 39
objections, 40–46
Olstrom, Elinor, 23n63, 127n13, 129
open fields, 68; compliance production in, 69. *See also* boundaries
ordinary citizens, 133–34
original confinement, 70

Pareto-optimality principle, 21, 37, 131
parliamentary committees, 107–8
Parsons, Talcott, 40, 46
persuasion, 56
Plato, 3, 4, 12
policy process, 132
polis, 2, 3n5, 4, 5, 6, 8
politeia, 4, 5
political action, 29–60; concept, 38; consequentiality, 40; defined, 39–40; directiveness, 38; as intentional action, 40; objections, 40–46. *See also* compliance; fields of political action
political behaviour, 29
political class, 133
political good, 127–29
politically relevant actors, 133
political motivation, 44
political obligations, enlargement of, 119
political warranty, 121
politics: as activities, 11–13; as aggregation, 21–24; as allocation, 19–21; as behavioural domain, 45; characterisation of, 125; components, 136; as conflict, 15–16; definition of, 125; dismembering of, 7–11; ethics and, 5; Greek conception of, 2–4; horizontal and vertical conceptions, 2–7; human interactions, 106; as institutional locus, 13–15; as pluridimensional process, 132; as power,

125–27; as production process, 118; as public good production, 127–29; as solution to social dilemmas, 129–32; as specific means, 16–19; study of, 10–11. *See also* compliance; governmental fields
politiké, 4
politikon, 5
politikos, 5
polyarchic polities, 107
population pressure circumscription, 70
power, 5–6, 125–27; coercion and, 16–19; as collective facility, 46; compliance and, 46–50; concept of, 46; as cultural hegemony, 46; love of, 41; Marxist conception of, 46; pleasure in, 42; as pure potential, 47–48; striving for, 41–42; as systemic property, 47; three-dimensional account of, 47; Weber on, 47
primitive circumscriptions, 71
private goods, 127
private obligation, 119–20; enlargement of, 119
property rights, 121
protection, 102, 118
public authority, 132–33; autonomy of struggle for, 137–39; competencies, 139; ordinary citizens, 133–34; political class, 133; politically relevant actors, 133
public bureaucracies, 95
public enforcer, 77
public goods, 127–29; private goods *vs.*, 127; production of, 120
pure potential, power as, 47

recognition respect, 33n14
regulations, 102, 118
Renaissance city-states, 6
resource concentration, 70
respect: appraisal, 33n14; recognition, 33n14; right to, 34, 35; worthy of, 33. *See also* honour
res publica, 5

rights: constitutionalisation of, 124; protection of, 140
right to respect, 34, 35
Rokkan, Stein, 65n10
Rousseau, J. J., 7, 84n39, 116
ruler/subject relationship, 72–87. *See also* accumulation of enforcement resources

sanctions, 54–55
Sartori, Giovanni, 10n19, 14, 14n32, 15, 24n64, 72
Schmitt, Carl, 10, 14, 16, 17, 86
Schumpeter, J. A., 21
Seeley, Robert, 85
Sejanus, Lucius Marcus, 41
self-interest, 36n19
self-organisation, 141
shame, 34
Simon, Herbert, 29
Smith, Adam, 8, 9, 119n2
social circumscription, 70
social dilemmas, 22–24, 129–32
social norms, 43
social relationship: closed towards exterior, 66; confinement of actors, 68–72; mode of interaction, 68; open towards exterior, 65–66
social reputation, 34
society, 8–9. *See also* civil society
sovereignty, 82–83
spatial understanding of politics, 14–15
state: civil society *vs.*, 8; exit and, 63; politics and, 6
Stoppino, Mario, 24n64, 38, 48n44, 54n52, 91n1, 102n18, 122, 125n10

Strauss, L., 10
synallagmatic relationship, 69, 120–22; acquisitions, 120–21; allocations resulting from, 121; among private persons, 121; exchanges, 111, 114

Tacitus, 41
third-party enforcement, 75–78, 80
Tingsten, Herbert, 29

ultimacy, 139–43
utility: concept, 36; imperial drive, 36–37; transforming motivation into, 37

values: authoritative allocation of, 20, 118; Eastonian perspective, 20; fields of political action and, 109–15, *114*; illegitimate acquisitions of, 119. *See also* goods
vertical conception of politics, 2–7. *See also* horizontal conception of politics
voice, 62; as request for compliance, 64; as residual of exit, 62–63; state organisations, 63
von Humbolt, W., 8n11

warranty. *See* political warranty
Warren, Mark E., 15–16, 19, 19n54, 24n64, 49n45, 126n11
Weber, Max, 14, 17, 41, 41n29, 47, 65–66
Weingast, R. Barry, 106n22
William of Moerbeke, 5
worthy of respect, 33

About the Author

Stefano Bartolini (1952) is Peter Mair Chair in Comparative Politics at the European University Institute, Florence. He has previously taught at the Universities of Florence, Trieste, Geneva, and Bologna. He was Director of the Robert Schuman Centre for Advanced Studies, Florence (2006–2013). His publications were awarded the Stein Rokkan UNESCO Prize (1990); the Gregory Luebbert APSA Prize (2001); the APSA European Politics Division Prize (2002); and the European Union Studies Association, Honourable Mention (2007).

www.ingramcontent.com/pod-product-compliance
Lightning Source LLC
Chambersburg PA
CBHW022014300426
44117CB00005B/185